Critical Guides to Fr

27 Montaigne: Essais

Critical Guides to French Texts

EDITED BY ROGER LITTLE, WOLFGANG VAN EMDEN, DAVID WILLIAMS

MONTAIGNE

Essais

John Holyoake

Lecturer in French,
University of Sheffield

Grant & Cutler Ltd
1983

I.S.B.N. 84-499-6742-2

DEPÓSITO LEGAL: V. 2.747-1983

Printed in Spain by
Artes Gráficas Soler, S.A., Valencia
for
GRANT & CUTLER LTD
11 BUCKINGHAM STREET, LONDON W.C.2

Contents

Contents

Introduction

This book about the *Essais* is similar to all short introductions to any great work in that it is only justifiable if it is designed and used as a supplement to rather than a substitute for a personal acquaintance with the work itself. It differs from similar works in that it goes on to propose that, since the *Essais* are unique in literature, they ought to be approached in a special way. It is written to meet some of the initial, practical needs of those who are about to read the *Essais* for the first time; it does not assume that they have unlimited time at their disposal nor that they already possess a cultural background sufficient to equip them to tackle a complex work written some four hundred years ago in a foreign tongue.

All the references to the *Essais* are taken from the following edition: Michel de Montaigne, *Essais*, edited by Alexandre Micha, 3 vols (Garnier-Flammarion, Paris, 1969). This is a cheap, convenient edition with a table of dates, an introduction and a short bibliography. It gives the essential indication of the successive layers of composition, has brief notes to explain references, translates the classical quotations and gives some of the more important variants. There is also a useful glossary.

References are indicated as follows: I, 8, p.70A. This means Book I chapter 8 page 70. The letter A denotes the date of composition, the significance of which is explained on page 13. The number in brackets after an author's name refers to the suggestions for further reading at the end of this book.

Introduction

This book about the Essays is meant to all superimmodifications to
any great work in that it is only useful and it is distance and
used as a supplement to rather than a substitute for the personal
acquaintance with the work itself. If differs from similar works
in this: it goes on to propose that, since the Essays are unique in
literature, they ought to be approached in a special way. It is
often found that some of the initial, practical needs of those who
first about to read the Essays for the first time or those that feeling
that they have unlimited time at their disposal, nor that they
already possess a cultural background sufficient to equip them
to tackle a complex work written some four hundred years ago
in a sort language.

All the references to the Essays are taken from the following
edition, *Michel de Montaigne, Essais*, edited by Alexandre
Micha, 3 vols (Garnier-Flammarion, Paris, 1969). This is a
cheap, convenient edition with a Table of dates, an introduction
and useful bibliography. It gives the essential indication of the
successive layers of composition, has index-notes to explain
references afterlife. The plan of annotations, and gives some of
the more important variants. It has also a useful glossary.

References are indicated as follows, i.e., iii, 3, 921. This means
Book I, chapter 3, page 921. The later 'A' denotes the date of
composition, the significance of which is explained on page (3).
The number in brackets after the author's name refers to the
suggestions for further reading, at the end of this book.

1. The Essais in the Context of Montaigne's Life

In a certain sense the *Essais* are an unconventional auto-biography, so it might appear unnecessary for this introduction to include an outline of the main features of Montaigne's life. Montaigne himself, however, disdains to give us a traditional or chronological account. Although it might seem presumptuous to know better than the author himself, a few basic facts give a context to many remarks in the *Essais* which otherwise might easily be misunderstood; they will also serve to show by contrast with the *Essais* the relative importance that Montaigne accords to the various external activities which occupied his life.

Montaigne was born in 1533 and died in 1592. Thus his adult life coincided with a period of religious strife and political manoeuvring which culminated in the savagery and corruption of the Religious Wars which raged virtually unabated from 1562 until after Montaigne's death. He was the eldest surviving son and heir of a prosperous Gascon family which had traded in fish and wine in Bordeaux until two or three generations previously, but which had signalled its gradual movement away from business and its desire to be associated with activities more appropriate to nobles by the purchase in 1477 of the château de Montaigne by Raymond Eyquem, our author's great-grand-father. Three generations later, Michel Eyquem de Montaigne was the first to drop the family name and call himself by the name of the estate he inherited. Montaigne's father spared no money or pain over his son's education: he was at first deliberately brought up amongst humble working folk and later had a private tutor who taught him Latin as his first language until the age of six. His formal schooling was at the prestigious *collège de Guyenne*, where his skill in Latin deteriorated in spite of some eminent tutors. Montaigne was shocked by the corporal punishment which was meted out because it was counter-productive educationally, risked causing permanent moral damage to the pupils and offended against his lifelong hatred of cruelty. We do not know much about Montaigne between the ages of thirteen and twenty-one when he left the *collège*, although many believe he studied law at the university of Toulouse.

His career as a magistrate may well have begun at a tax-court in Périgueux and he was certainly a member of the court (*parlement*) in Bordeaux from 1557-70. During these years (1559-63), he formed a deep friendship with a legal colleague, La Boétie, a classical scholar and poet, whose early death in 1563 made a lasting impression on him. At thirty-two, he entered into an arranged marriage with Françoise de la Chassaigne, whose family had long been established in Bordeaux. Six girls were born of the marriage but only one, Léonor, survived more than a few months. In 1569, in response to his father's request, Montaigne published his translation from Latin of Raimond Sebond's *Book of Creatures, or Natural Theology* in which the author tries to prove the truth of Christianity by reasoned arguments derived from the evidence of creation.

After failing to get promotion to one of the higher courts in the *parlement*, Montaigne sold his position in 1570 when he was thirty-seven. In the following year he retired from the trials of public life and looked forward to the peace and freedom to be found in the pursuit of leisure by having a Latin inscription to that effect painted on a wall in the tower of his château where his library was installed. Within a year or so he had begun work on his *Essais*. His retirement did not in the least imply that he cut his contacts with the world at large. The frequent trips that he had made to Paris during his legal career meant that he was already far from being a blinkered provincial. Between 1572-76, for example, he made a number of unavailing attempts to bring the duc de Guise and Henri de Navarre together at court. The writing which he had been doing in the nine years since his retirement was published early in 1580 as what we now know as Books I and II of the *Essais*. Montaigne was then forty-seven. In the same year he set off on a fifteen month long journey through Germany, Switzerland and Austria to Italy. The ostensible purpose was to take the waters at various spas in an attempt to alleviate the pain caused by the kidney stone which he first felt acutely in 1578 and which intermittently caused him a great deal of pain for the rest of his life. Other factors behind the journey were his evident love of travel, a longing to see Venice and Rome plus a desire to escape from the routine of domestic affairs. Montaigne kept a record of his travels which was not intended for publication but it was, in fact, published in 1774 as a *Journal de voyage*.

Whilst absent on his travels he was elected mayor of Bordeaux as his father had been. Montaigne's disinclination to serve was countered when Henri III himself wrote to command him to take up this responsibility. Unusually he was re-elected for a second term. The first was comparatively peaceful but the second, 1583-85, was not. In striving to keep Bordeaux loyal to the king, Montaigne had to contend with strong Protestant forces in the immediate surroundings and with a faction of extreme Catholics (*ligueurs*) within. Plague was also a problem in the later stages of his period of office.

In 1586, Protestants and *ligueurs* were still fighting a few miles from the château; there was some pillaging and harrassment on his lands and Montaigne felt under suspicion from both sides since he had friendly links with both. Finally, he was forced to leave the château for six months with his family and retinue to escape from the plague. On his return, Henri de Navarre, the Protestant leader, spent a night at the château in 1587 (he had also been in 1584). In 1588, Montaigne was further involved in negotiations between Henri III and Henri de Navarre, trying to bring them into an alliance against the *Ligue*. During this period he was imprisoned in the Bastille by the *ligueurs* until Catherine de Medici, the queen mother, intervened to secure an early release. Another reason for Montaigne's absence from the château in 1588 was that he had to attend to another edition of the *Essais* with the addition of Book III.

In the four remaining years of his life, he continued to work on the *Essais* as illness confined him more and more to the château. He died of quinsy in 1592. Further details can be found in Frame's biography (3) upon which the preceding account is largely based.

Most of the features of this outline of his life find their echoes in the *Essais* but almost always with an unusual twist or with unexpected weighting. Biographical information of this sort can only help to explain in what sense the *Essais* are autobiographical if it is used with great care. There is little in what we have seen so far to lead us to expect the unique and subtle qualities of the *Essais*, the work on which Montaigne's reputation is based, for his letters, his translation and the *Journal de voyage* are of secondary importance only.

The best way to begin to grasp the uniqueness of the *Essais* is to be clear about the way in which they were composed, because this gives an invaluable insight into their essential features.

When the first edition was published in 1580 in Bordeaux, the *Essais* consisted of two books of fifty-seven and thirty-seven chapters respectively. They had been written, we remember, over a period of some nine years. The details of the second, third and (possibly) fourth editions need not concern us except that we should note that the second includes the first evidence of Montaigne's tendency towards making interpolations. After his long journey abroad, he felt a need to intercalate into his original text a series of additions which recorded his subsequent experiences. These additions were not merely added on to the existing text at the end or in any easily indentifiable spot; they were inserted wherever Montaigne thought they should be fitted in, thus masking the chronological development.

The fifth edition of 1588 is of great importance: unlike the first two editions it was published in Paris (possibly a sign of the author's greater confidence?) and consisted of a completely new third book of thirteen chapters together with some six hundred additions to Books I and II. Montaigne thus continued on a more massive scale the process of interpolation evident in the second edition.

In the four years which remained before his death in 1592, Montaigne continued to make further additions to his *Essais*. The fascinating point about his work at this stage, however, is that although he almost certainly had a sixth edition in mind, he wrote no completely new chapters. He preferred to make some one thousand additions, sometimes of only a word or two, sometimes of several pages. These post-1588 additions, representing about one quarter of the total work, were made in the margins of his own 1588 edition (possibly unbound), or sometimes, where space did not allow, on slips of paper which were to be pasted in at the appropriate place indicated by insertion marks. This document, known as the *exemplaire de Bordeaux*, is the basis for most modern editions.

To be aware of this process of composition by accretion is not merely a pedantic concern for detail; it gives a vital clue to Montaigne's methods, purposes and fundamental beliefs. The various layers of the *Essais* which were gradually built up over the twenty odd years from 1571 to 1592 recorded the shifts and changes in Montaigne's thoughts; the fact that he preferred to intercalate and juxtapose his later reflections against his earlier ones rather than to excise or to correct them is an indication that he was more concerned to record the changing patterns of his thought processes than to present any fixed or definitive state-ment of a point of view. The transient quality of his opinions and the elusiveness of his personality represented more nearly, he thought, the truth about himself than permanently held beliefs or an artificially constructed immutability of character.

This feature of the composition of the *Essais* is of such consequence that modern editors give an indication in the text of the period to which individual passages belong. The most convenient way for us to refer to the three separate periods in this study is by the letters A, B and C according to the following principles:

A for passages first published in 1580 and written between 1571-80
B for passages first published in 1588 and written between 1580-88
C for passages first published in 1595 and written between 1588-92
1595 was the date of the first posthumous publication of the *Essais* which contained the C passages.

When we look at a chapter in Book I or II, therefore, we need to remember that what we are reading may have been written over a time span of some twenty years. It may also just be worth noting in passing that nobody can really be certain whether each of the earliest passages was written at a single sitting. Dating of the earliest sections in Books I and II is extremely complex; in broad terms, such sections fall either into an early group written between 1571-74 or a later one written between 1577-80.

Another factor which makes the *Essais* less than straight-forward is the order in which the chapters have been placed by Montaigne in the first two books. Although most chapters in Book I were written in the earlier period mentioned above and most in Book II in the later period, there are plenty of exceptions to this. Chapters 1-6 in Book II, for example, were written in the earlier period, while the opening chapter in Book I and several others in the group from 26-31 are from the later period.

The length of chapters varies enormously: Montaigne began writing chapters of no more than a page or so and gradually made them longer as time went on but he never settled into any pattern of normal length. Perhaps a more significant factor to bear constantly in mind is that no single chapter encompasses all that Montaigne had to say on any subject which he considered important. His habit of constantly returning to his favourite themes is one which we shall look at more closely later. In a way, this habit is connected with another which is not obvious to the modern reader: Montaigne did not break the flow of his composition by dividing it into paragraphs — these divisions have been introduced by later editors.

In spite of some unusual features, then, the *Essais* achieved a solid success in the sixteenth century, as repeated new editions demonstrate. The qualities for which his contemporaries admired him (his stoicism and his ability to turn a sententious phrase, for example) are not necessarily identical to those for which he is most generally valued today. Paradoxically, his contemporaries admired him in spite of several characteristics (the self-portrait, the loose structure, for example) which we today would judge to be among the most original. An investigation of the early phases of Montaigne's composition will set us on the path to discovering the essential nature of the *Essais*.

2. *The Composition of the* Essais

How did Montaigne come to write the *Essais* and how did their
purpose evolve? We know that Montaigne was a voracious
reader and that he possessed a library of impressive proportions
for a private individual in the sixteenth century. He himself tells
us that, because of his poor memory, he was in the habit of
jotting comments in the margins and on the spare pages at the
beginning and end of books. Later he transcribed some of these
annotations to form part of the body of the *Essais* (II, 10,
p.89A). From an examination of the earliest chapters we can see
that, at that stage, Montaigne's writing was an amalgam of
anecdotes illustrating practical moral problems interspersed with
quotations and a very occasional personal comment. The initial
stimulus to write appears to have been either a contemporary
incident or a conversation or, most often, his own reading. The
compilation of anecdotes followed by a brief moral comment,
often culled from the literature of the ancient world, was within
a well established tradition and was a part of the process of
dissemination of the newly recovered wisdom of antiquity. The
grouping together of historical examples of behaviour (*exempla*)
followed by pithy reflections on the human condition
(*sententiae*) in 'common-place books', was a ready-made format
for Montaigne's early attempts at composition. The subject
matter mostly involved some aspect of human behaviour (often
of a paradoxical or inconsistent nature) either in the area of
military operations (for example, how far is it honourable to
deceive an enemy in war?) or diplomatic relations or in the wider
context of questions which he merely broaches at this stage but
to which he returned frequently later, such as fear, death,
suicide, life's unpredictability, the variability of human nature.

In one of his earliest direct comments on the reasons why he began to write, Montaigne describes it as a sort of therapy necessary to curb the exuberant activities of his mind after his retirement. He had expected his mind to become more composed if there was less to occupy it from outside. Instead, as he describes in powerfully metaphorical language:

> faisant le cheval eschappé, il [= mon esprit] se donne cent fois plus d'affaire à soy mesmes, qu'il n'en prenoit pour autruy; et m'enfante tant de chimeres et monstres fantasques les uns sur les autres, sans ordre et sans propos, que pour en contempler à mon aise l'ineptie et l'estrangeté, j'ay commancé de les mettre en rolle, esperant avec le temps luy en faire honte à luy mesmes. (I, 8, p.70A)

As time went on and as the chapters lengthened, the mosaic of second-hand opinion gradually changed in character. The personal comments became increasingly more important until, in some cases, they predominated over the other material. By this stage, Montaigne was ready to treat subjects such as pain and death, virtue and ambition, education and retirement, not only at greater length but also with a different focus; to the personal comments that he made about such general subjects he added description of his own experiences as examples. When he came to write the preface to the first edition, Montaigne could say that a self-portrait was his objective. 'Je veus qu'on m'y voie en ma façon simple, naturelle et ordinaire, sans contantion et artifice: car c'est moy que je peins... Ainsi, lecteur, je suis moy-mesmes la matiere de mon livre' (Au lecteur).

Viewed within the time span of the twenty years from 1572-92, the increasingly personal nature of the contents is plain to see. Self-portraiture is more important in B passages than in A and still more important in C passages than in B. In recent years, critics have tended to argue that even in the earliest chapters there are quite clear indications of Montaigne's personality. This is an entirely desirable tendency because it is easy to exaggerate the impersonality of the early chapters but we must remind ourselves that Montaigne himself admitted that 'de mes premiers essays, aucuns puent un peu à l'estranger' (III, 5, p.90B).

It is not difficult to see how the simple process of recording thoughts and reactions as they passed through the mind could lead to the wider aim of self-portraiture, especially when Montaigne realised that his opinions were constantly changing. Soon there came a crucial discovery: his opinions were valuable not so much in themselves but because they were his. In writing his *Essais* he could study himself. The fundamental paradox is that the subject of the *Essais*, Montaigne himself, is at once so obvious and yet so extraordinary; nobody had written about himself in this way ever before.

Montaigne is nearly always ambiguous when he refers to his 'sotte entreprise' which is 'si esloigné de l'usage commun' (II, 8, p.56A). Claiming that he first began to write to escape from the melancholy which followed his retirement, he complains that 'me trovant entierement despourveu et vuide de toute autre matiere, je me suis presenté moy-mesmes à moy, pour argument et pour subject'. When he first wrote those words he went on to talk of his 'dessein farouche et extravagant' but when he came to make a C addition, the *Essais* are described as 'le seul livre au monde de son espece'.

By the time that Montaigne began to speak directly about his desire for perfect communication — for perfect self-revelation — it is remarkable how unequivocal, how urgent, is the language he uses.

> Je suis affamé de me faire connoistre; et ne me chaut à combien, pourveu que ce soit veritablement; ou, pour dire mieux, je n'ay faim de rien, mais je crains mortellement d'estre pris en eschange par ceux à qui il arrive de connoistre mon nom. (III, 5, p.62B)

> Je ne laisse rien à desirer et deviner de moy. Si on doibt s'en entretenir, je veux que ce soit veritablement et justement. Je reviendrois volontiers de l'autre monde pour démentir celuy qui me formeroit autre que je n'estois, fut-ce pour m'honorer. (III, 9, p.196B)

When statements such as these are added to Montaigne's

persistent attacks on hypocrisy in general, it becomes obvious that we have touched on a theme which requires some explanation. The simplest explanation of the desire for perfect self-revelation is the historical one — Montaigne was so revolted by the double-dealing and corruption inherent in the Religious Wars that he wished to isolate himself as far as possible from such deception. Montaigne himself offered another explanation: he claims that he found it impossible to lie consistently because of his poor memory. This conceals more than it reveals because the evidence of the *Essais* proves that even if Montaigne's memory was poor in a certain sense, there is much more to be said on the subject. In any case, such a practical explanation is insufficient to justify the intensity of the need for total self-revelation. Another line of approach has been to see the *Essais* as a substitute for the ideal friendship which was lost on the death of La Boétie.

While all these explanations have an element of truth, they are all partial. Nearer the truth, because it is more capable of subsuming others, is the idea that self-revelation is an attempt by Montaigne to make objective what he feared might be irredeemably subjective. Given the elusive, evanescent qualities which Montaigne attributed to human personality, it is understandable that he might seek to give permanence and solidity to his own in the only way he could, through the medium of art. Ultimately we shall see that this objective is bound up with various key aspects of Montaigne's vision of the world: his distrust of abstract, general truths, his hatred of dogmatism, his view of the world as being in a constant state of flux and ruled by chance, his many-sided approach to all problems. Against this background, there was one area in which Montaigne saw some hope of approaching a limited certainty, some possibility of stability amid the shifts and changes of the 'branloire perenne' (III, 2, p.20B). This was the study of himself. Whatever its advantages, however, self-study remained subjective and was essentially temporal. If he could break out of the prison of his own subjectivity by communicating his essence to a reader, he might achieve a vicarious sense of objectivity and of permanence. The man who was often so concerned to

preserve his independence thus accepted this huge dependence
on his reader. It is factors such as these which take us to the
heart of the *Essais* and which explain the intensity of the
language whenever Montaigne broaches the subject of self-
revelation.

The self-imposed task was a difficult one. Quite apart from
the contemporary suspicion of such an enterprise in principle,
there are wider conventions governing the sort of things one
might say about oneself (self-praise, even where justified, might
be frowned upon, for example). In addition, there is the
problem of intimate details which are not normally discussed.
Such difficulties caused Montaigne few problems. Far from
running away from them, he disarms the reader by his matter-
of-fact approach and his complete confidence that nothing
which is part of a man's whole being is unsuitable for
description or discussion.

A more substantial problem is caused by the nature of human
personality itself. As seen by Montaigne it is elusive, constantly
changing under internal and external influences.

> Non seulement le vent des accidens me remue selon son
> inclination, mais en outre je me remue et trouble moy
> mesme par l'instabilité de ma posture... Si je parle
> diversement de moy, c'est que je me regarde diversement...
> quiconque s'estudie bien attentifvement trouve en soy...
> cette volubilité et discordance. Je n'ay rien à dire de moy,
> entierement, simplement et solidement, sans confusion et
> sans meslange, ny en un mot. (II, 1, pp.8-9B)

In the second half of this quotation, Montaigne makes it quite
clear that he is fully aware of the problems of self-revelation. A
further complication is that the act of becoming sufficiently
aware of one's own psychological processes involves the
modification of what one originally intended to describe.
Montaigne was well aware of the interaction, the symbiotic
relationship between himself and the *Essais*.

Me peignant pour autruy, je me suis peint en moy de

couleurs plus nettes que n'estoyent les miennes premieres.
Je n'ay pas plus faict mon livre que mon livre m'a faict,
livre consubstantiel à son autheur, d'une occupation
propre, membre de ma vie. (II, 18, p.326C)

What he had already written about himself limited his freedom
because he did not wish to falsify his words. 'Je sens ce proffit
inesperé de la publication de mes meurs qu'elle me sert
aucunement de regle' (III, 9, p.193B). Similarly, the knowledge
that he was ultimately to record his actions might restrict his
freedom since he would not wish to do what he would not
willingly record. 'Qui s'obligeroit à tout dire, s'obligeroit à ne
rien faire de ce qu'on est contraint de taire' (III, 5, p.60C). In
addition to the problems caused by the interaction between
Montaigne and the *Essais* there was the third factor — the
reader. Montaigne's desire to be known perfectly caused a
dilemma: if he represented the labyrinthine complexity of
himself in all its detail and inconsistency, the reader would be
confused; if he simplified to ensure understanding, he would not
be faithful to himself. Montaigne knew that in the pursuit of his
'dessein farouche et extravagant' he might be led into obscurity
which, he said 'à parler en bon escient, je hay bien fort, et
l'éviterois si je me sçavois eviter' (III, 9, p.209B).

There is more to be said about the contention that the central
purpose of the *Essais* is to create a self-portrait of the author;
for one thing, Montaigne is not totally consistent in pursuing
this objective. Yet this central purpose should remain constantly
in our minds as we read the *Essais* and reflect on the meaning. In
doing this we shall be following Montaigne's own advice and
remembering that it was not primarily for the ideas he expressed
in them that he valued the *Essais*.

Qui sera en cherche de science, si la pesche où elle se loge: il
n'est rien dequoy je face moins de profession. Ce sont icy
mes fantasies, par lesquelles je ne tasche point à donner à
connoistre les choses, mais moy.... Ainsi je ne pleuvy
aucune certitude, si ce n'est de faire connoistre jusques à
quel poinct monte, pour cette heure, la connoissance que

j'en ay. Qu'on ne s'attende pas aux matieres, mais à la
façon que j'y donne. (II, 10, p.78A)

However, nothing is ever quite as straightforward as it seems
with Montaigne; there is sometimes a difference between what
he says and what he does. Although he rarely takes up an overtly
didactic stance, it is clear that, as his confidence in his own
powers grew, he felt not only the need to communicate what he
discovered about himself in the course of his introspection, but
also that his self-knowledge might benefit others, since all men
are cast in the same mould in spite of their differences.

Je propose une vie basse et sans lustre, c'est tout un. On
attache aussi bien toute la philosophie morale à une vie
populaire et privée que à une vie de plus rich estoffe;
chaque homme porte la forme entiere de l'humaine
condition. (III, 2, p.20B)

Grafted on to his major preoccupation with self-revelation, in
spite of denials and repeated criticism of his own competence,
Montaigne evidently came to believe that he could be read with
profit by those who knew what to look for and how to find it in
the *Essais*.

3. *Approaches to the* Essais

Now that we have seen something of how and why Montaigne wrote the *Essais* we must turn our attention to how we can best approach them ourselves. The discussion falls into two parts. The first deals with tactics for overcoming possible difficulties over Montaigne's language; the second discusses a strategy for dealing with an unusual text consisting of three volumes of over eleven hundred pages divided into one hundred and seven assorted chapters.

Those who already have some experience of reading sixteenth-century texts in French may well omit the first section on language. Those who genuinely prefer to tackle the challenge of the unknown without help will not be reading these words anyhow, but for those who would like to consider a few hints which have saved many readers time in the past and which may enhance enjoyment and increase understanding, the pages on 'How to read the *Essais*' might suggest a strategy adaptable according to personal taste and requirements.

*　　　*　　　*　　　*

These remarks are addressed to those readers whose native language is not French who might welcome a few words about the shock of unfamiliarity they may experience when they first read the *Essais*.

One soon grows accustomed to the unusual spellings: the use of *y* for *i* as in 'j'ay' or 'vray'; the extra *s* in words like 'mesmes', 'esté', and 'esloigné'; *oi* instead of *ai* in 'connoissance', 'foible'; *-oit* for *-ait* in imperfect tense endings; *ez* for *é* as in 'qualitez' and so on. Most modern editions now have some apparatus to explain the meaning of words and phrases which have gone out of usage and are not to be found in standard modern dictionaries. More importantly, they also deal with words which are familiar but which had different meanings in the sixteenth century: for example, 'curieusement' = 'soigneusement', 'science' = 'connaissance', 'aucunement' = 'un peu'. English readers will be pleasantly surprised that some of the notes (which are primarily for the French) prove to be unnecessary for them since they will translate the text quite easily without being disturbed by the difference between sixteenth century and modern usage: 'creance', 'douloir', 'suasion', 'ire', pose few problems for an alert linguist. The generally looser rules of sixteenth-century syntax, the occasionally different rules of grammar (different genders, for example) will be unlikely to upset the English reader.

In many editions, while notes deal with the more difficult and unusual vocabulary difficulties, there is a glossary for words and phrases which occur more frequently. It is well worth while making a conscious effort to commit some of them to memory in the early stages (there are under four pages of them in the Garnier-Flammarion edition) because it saves a lot of time in the long run and increases confidence and enjoyment very swiftly. Finally when particular words seem to be of crucial importance and it appears worth while doing a little exploration in specialist dictionaries, Huguet and Cotgrave[1] can be very useful.

Even when all these aids are sensibly employed, however, there is no denying that, in the early stages at least, the best way to proceed is with a good modern translation ready to hand for consultation side by side with Montaigne's text. There is nothing to be ashamed of in the use of a translation provided it is used wisely. My only plea, but a crucial one (because of the beauty of Montaigne's language amongst other reasons), would be that the French should always, without exception, be read together with the translation. Most readers soon find that they can wean themselves from the translation and have recourse to it less and less as they become more familiar with the text. After a while, of course, it is only necessary to consult the translation in cases of

[1] E. Huguet, *Dictionnaire de la langue française du seizième siècle*, 7 vols (Didier, Champion, Paris, 1925-32, 1946-67).
R. Cotgrave, *A dictionarie of the French and English tongues*, reproduced from the first edition, London, 1611 (Columbia University of South Carolina Press, 1950, second printing 1968).

real difficulty. By the time the reader is acute enough to perceive that the translator does not always get it quite right, the translation has done its work. My personal preference is for Donald Frame's version (*11*).

*   *   *   *

We can now return to a question which stems from our knowledge about the different layers of composition in the *Essais*. How does one read the *Essais*? From what has been said about the method of composition the answer is not self-evident. Should they be tackled chronologically? There are two aspects to this. Should the chapters be read in the order in which they appear in the books or in the order of composition or in some other order? In the case of individual chapters, should one read straight through or read A sections first followed by B and then C? The justification for such an approach would presumably be to follow as closely as possible the chronological development of Montaigne's composition. The trouble with this, apart from the difficulty of dating the chapters, is that there is no easy or certain way of dating the material written before 1580 nor of knowing exactly the order of composition of the B and C additions. Any attempt, therefore, at a chronological approach is bound to be only partially successful and is not recommended for a first reading.

The most practical way to read the *Essais* is to take the chapter as the basic unit; it is, after all, the one Montaigne himself chose to present to the reader. A chapter in Book I or Book II as published in 1588 would have had additions inserted but not differentiated. However, it is most desirable that a firm note be taken of the three phases of writing. This can be done without rigorously excluding B and C passages, but by consciously registering that they were written at a different time. It is a good idea to acquire some experience of reading the layers in chronological order on re-reading any chapter found to be particularly interesting or indicated for special attention.

Should the chapters be read in the order of their appearance in the published editions? This is a matter of personal preference.

The strongest argument in favour of such an approach is that Montaigne, for whatever reasons, published them like that. Yet it is a fact that the shortest chapters (sometimes a single page), many of which Montaigne placed early in Book I, are among the least immediately appealing. I would not hesitate to recommend a reader to move swiftly on to the longer, meatier chapters, after only a brief taste of the shortest ones. On the whole, the earliest chapters are more rewarding when they are fitted into the broader pattern of Montaigne's work. No harm is done by going back to them at a later stage of study. The most obvious chapters in Book I to start with are numbers 8, 14, 20, 21, 23, 25, 26, 28, 31, 39. Similar problems are posed by Book II, although there are fewer chapters of under five pages. Among the more substantial here are numbers 8, 11, 16, 17, 37. The real problem in Book II is the massive twelfth chapter called the *Apologie* which has some one hundred and sixty pages. A special section later in this book has been devoted to the *Apologie* and the reader should be in a better position to decide when and how to tackle it after reading that section. Only one chapter in Book III is under ten pages; all are interesting although obviously some are more important than others. The book can be read chronologically or according to taste.

We have already seen that no single chapter contains an exhaustive treatment of any of Montaigne's major themes. This poses something of a problem for a reader who at some stage tries to assemble evidence scattered throughout the *Essais* with a view to working out what Montaigne's ideas were on any particular topic. Merely to be aware of the problem before starting to study the *Essais* suggests a partial solution. It is possible to save an enormous amount of time if, even on the first reading, one is prepared to make a note of page references when Montaigne deals with his major themes. Brief indications of some of these are given below to help in the initial stages:

death/illness/pain/doctors
Stoicism/Scepticism/hedonism/self-fulfilment
judgement/memory; reason/knowledge/wisdom/education
private and public life/ambition/serenity of mind

links between mind and body/psychological comments
customs and relativity
virtue/innate goodness/self-improvement
friendship/personal relationships/women
religion/superstition/intolerance/cruelty
chance/diversity/changeability
the art and pleasures of reading/composition
intellectual dishonesty

Finally, a great deal of time can be saved if one is forewarned about a number of characteristics of Montaigne's way of thinking, which fundamentally affect the way he writes. The reader will have to take these on trust for the moment; in checking their validity against his own experience of the *Essais* the reader will be going to the heart of Montaigne's attempt to convey his essence. We might briefly describe the most important as follows. He has the sort of mind which refuses to simplify; he loves to break down tidy, conventional explanations and find exceptions; almost involuntarily, any proposition will provoke a reaction which leads him to explore the possible validity of its opposite; sometimes his ability to see another person's point of view is so highly developed that Montaigne says he cannot subsequently distinguish between it and his own. He is fascinated by ideas for their own sake; he can be so struck by an idea that he begins to toy with it, to explore its implications as if he were wilfully daring it to lead him to paradoxical or unorthodox conclusions. Montaigne admits that he can become so involved in the subject in hand that he can be carried away by the momentum of the argument itself. Then there is Montaigne's inability (or lack of desire) to reach a definite conclusion; this is the obverse of his refusal to simplify. It is a quality which is bound up, as we shall see, with his whole attitude to scepticism and to the complexity of life. In its most extreme form, it can result in Montaigne adopting someone else's point of view in order to avoid uncertainty in a situation in which choice is necessary but agonisingly difficult.

Now that we have seen something of the way in which the *Essais* were composed, how their purpose evolved and how some

of the practical difficulties in approaching the work might be
tackled, we are ready to look more closely at the qualities of
Montaigne's composition.

4. *Form and Style in the* Essais

We shall look at the form and style of the *Essais* before examining the ideas (which are normally dealt with first) for the following reasons. However important the ideas in the *Essais* may be, Montaigne's avowed intention was to compose a self-portrait, a task which posed technical problems, some of which we have already touched on in Chapter Two. One of the great fascinations of reading the *Essais* is to see how Montaigne sought to fashion a literary form capable of coping with the complex task he had set himself. When self-portraiture matured into a broader task of seeking to cast light on the relationships between all men, the technical task became more complex still.

In what ways have the form and style of the *Essais* been conditioned by Montaigne's objectives? By form here, I mean the way in which books and chapters have been constructed; by style, all those elements of writing we shall look at in this chapter which constitute the two larger units just mentioned. In spite of some lofty disclaimers, Montaigne was preoccupied with questions of form and style; the *Essais* are full of his comments on them.

When commenting on style in others, Montaigne says: 'Je ne dicts pas que c'est bien dire, je dicts que c'est bien penser' (III, 5, p.88B). This implies the inseparability of form and content. One of the features which make the *Essais* so special is that there is the further inseparability of the book and the man, or as Montaigne so memorably expressed it: 'Icy, nous allons conformément et tout d'un trein, mon livre et moy. Ailleurs, on peut recommander et accuser l'ouvrage à part de l'ouvrier; icy non: qui touche l'un, touche l'autre' (III, 2, p.21B). Montaigne's passionate commitment to his task is frequently attested but never more so than in his search for a perfect form to convey his essence. Since even this formulation implies separation, it may be preferable to speak of the simultaneous invention of a new literary genre and a new content to go with it.

Before passing to a more detailed examination of the parts of the *Essais* we should pause over the title. When it appeared in 1580, the word *Essais* was virtually unprecedented and probably original in the sense that Montaigne used it. But what, indeed, was that sense? First, let us clear up a minor point: is it proper to call an individual chapter an *essai* since Montaigne calls them *chapitres*? Up to 1588 the title of the whole work was *Essais* and it was only in the posthumous edition of 1595 that it became *Les Essais*. Montaigne's own title is thus more modest than that of his editors. Most of Montaigne's early use of the word *essai* in the text implies a 'trying out' or 'testing out' with the connotation that the results are immature because they are only the first of many: 'Quant aux facultez naturelles qui sont en moy, dequoy c'est icy l'essay' (I, 26, p.194A. See also I, 50, p.357A; II, 10, p.387A; II, 17, p.316A). Another slightly different meaning can be deduced from Montaigne's description of the whole work as 'un registre des essais de ma vie' (III, 13, p.289B), where it is closer to the richer idea associated with the title word of the vital final chapter, 'experience'. Thus, although he clearly links the word with the process of self-discovery and self-revelation, he does not unequivocally use it to denote a new genre (the nearest he comes to this is in I, 40, p.303C and III, 9, p.205B).

To explore how far Montaigne was influenced by existing genres would take us too far afield. Let us briefly note in passing that Montaigne was no doubt familiar with and employed some of the techniques associated with a number of established genres including the discourse (a collection of an author's reflections on a variety of subjects), the letter and the dialogue. Montaigne did not limit himself to any one of these forms presumably because he judged that, in spite of their undoubted flexibility, none would provide him with a suitable vehicle for his particular project. Since the content was to be distinctive, the form had to be developed to match it.

Form

Montaigne's deep concern for both form and style should not
lead us to assume that his attitudes are unambiguous nor that his
practice and his theory are a perfect match. His comments on
the form of the *Essais* swing between two extremes: sometimes
he stresses the absence of form, or indeed, of any sense of order,
while elsewhere he claims there is a profound unity in all his
writing:

> Que sont-ce icy aussi, à la verité, que crotesques et corps
> monstrueux, rappiecez de divers membres, sans certaine
> figure, n'ayants ordre, suite ny proportion que fortuite? (I,
> 28, p.231A)

> Je m'esgare, mais plustost par licence que par mesgarde.
> Mes fantasies se suyvent, mais par fois c'est de loing, et se
> regardent, mais d'une veuë oblique. (III, 9, p.207B; see
> also p.177C and III, 5, p.91B)

In view of the process of composition by accretion it might
not seem surprising if there were some sense of disorder, some
brusque juxtapositions, indeed, that the *Essais* might be
properly described by Montaigne's own disparaging expressions
such as 'une marqueterie mal jointe' (III, 9, p.177C) or 'une
galimafrée de divers articles' (I, 46, p.331A). He dubbed as
'ennuyeuse' Cicero's elaborate structuring of his material: 'Car
ses prefaces, definitions, partitions, etymologies, consument la
plus part de son ouvrage' (II, 10, p.84A). Yet Montaigne insists
that, while the more customary forms of order may be missing,
there is a more fundamental unity in his own work: 'Mon livre
est tousjours un' (III, 9, p.177B). He, at least, is clear about
what binds together the apparently diverse parts and it is
'l'indiligent lecteur qui pert mon subject, non pas moy' (III, 9,
p.208C).

Books

How far does the theory match the practice? There is very little in the way of thematic organisation in the fifty-seven chapters in Book I and the thirty-seven in Book II. The most plausible attempt to discern a sort of structure has been by Sayce (*1*, pp.263-65). Without doubt there are links of sorts between certain chapters, although their nature varies in his analysis. A chapter may have some explicit link with the previous one (e.g. I, 5 and 6; 25 and 26; 39 and 40), or there may be an implicit thematic link (e.g. I, 19 and 20; 31 and 32); a refinement on this is when a long chapter follows a short one on the same theme or the reverse (I, 42 and 43; 39 and 40). Sometimes a central theme of a chapter may become a subsidiary theme of the following one or alternate chapters may be linked in some way. Not all of these links are demonstrably deliberate although it is true that Montaigne originally intended to have a chapter connected with La Boétie as the numerical centre-piece of the fifty-seven chapters of Book I (chapter 29 introduced by chapter 28, see p.231). What is more, we know that Montaigne deliberately placed at the beginning of the *Essais* a chapter which was not among his earliest compositions because it stressed uncertainty and diversity, thus setting the tone for an important theme in Books I and II. Similarly, the final lines of chapter 37 of Book II bring the discussion back to the theme of diversity in a deliberate echo of the opening chapter. It is rather more difficult to show grouping of chapters in Book II than in Book I (although 16-18, 33 and 34, 35 and 36 do have obvious links), and even more difficult in Book III. Villey (*4*, p.399) believed the chapters in Book III were arranged in the order of their composition.

Even if one accepts that all of the examples quoted show evidence of some concern with organisation, the chapters involved constitute only a small proportion of the total number either on the basis of individual books or the *Essais* as a whole. If there is a unifying plan we must look for it elsewhere.

Of course, one might simply say that the unifying factor throughout the *Essais* is Montaigne's own personality. This is true up to a point but it is possible to go further (even perhaps to

follow the author's wishes more closely) and to try to flesh out
this rather bare explanation. The key to this is not to look
myopically for relationships exclusively between consecutive
chapters. If one stands back just a little the answer is blindingly
obvious. The essential links between all the chapters, links to
which Montaigne himself surely referred in the comments we
saw earlier (p.30), are to be found in the network of Montaigne's
recurrent themes.

One of the principal features of Montaigne's writing is the
way in which he invariably returns, time and again, whatever his
ostensible starting point, to a set of recognisable favourite
themes. Although it is obviously difficult to define them, any
attentive reader soon recognises these fundamental preoccupations of Montaigne's mind. I am thinking of clusters of
themes such as the eternal problems of pain, death, health and
illness; the inseparability of mind and body, psychological
insights through introspection leading to self-knowledge; the
search for certainty, order and serenity in a world of shifting
values and endless diversity; the attraction of custom and
tradition but the dislike of all that impinges on personal freedom
and choice; the essential ingredients of the good life and the
nature of happiness; the problem of balancing personal
inclination with virtuous behaviour; the nature of commitment,
ambition and reputation; the nature and purpose of knowledge,
the role of reason, judgement, memory in education and in the
pursuit of morality; the dangers of intellectual dishonesty; the
need for practical results on the human scale rather than
theoretical, untestable speculation; the relative importance of
physical and spiritual attraction, friendship, love and marriage.
This list cannot be exhaustive; it is obviously impossible to
suggest briefly the subtle changes and the rich complexities
which emerge as these recurrent themes weave in and out of the
texture of the *Essais*. Their presence is a dominant factor in
ensuring the underlying unity, that sense of a seamless structure
and that familiar, distinctive resonance which is such a hall-
mark of the *Essais*. It can hardly be denied that their presence
sometimes leads to repetition, inconsistency, contradictions and
even disorder; but their inherent and enduring importance for all

who are interested in the human condition is a guarantee against the charges of monotony or triviality.

Chapters

The next largest unit in the *Essais* is the chapter. In broad terms, most of the early chapters are very short: about forty in Book I and sixteen in Book II have five pages or fewer in the Garnier-Flammarion edition, and this often includes additions to the original. Subsequently, Montaigne made a conscious decision to increase the length of his chapters (III, 9, p.209C). Each of the first two books has one chapter of over twenty and one of over thirty pages, while Book III has three of over twenty and three of over fifty. None of these compares with the *Apologie* with over one hundred and sixty pages. Montaigne never made a decision about the ideal length of a chapter. In a real sense, no chapter can be said to be complete since it was apparently Montaigne's intention to go on adding to them indefinitely. Perhaps the most crucial single fact about their structure is that they are conceived in such a way as to convey the spontaneous qualities of Montaigne's thought processes, to show his thoughts as they occurred to him and to be capable of infinite modification.

These general characteristics are perhaps the most important to keep in mind when one considers individual chapters since each can be said to have its own form. On the other hand, it is worth noting a number of broad characteristics which will illustrate the inventiveness of Montaigne's approach.

The earliest chapters are often little more than a general statement illustrated by a number of examples (I, 5, 6, 7, 15 for instance). Though some are very impersonal compared with later chapters, they are by no means devoid of personal comment (I, 8). Before long the chapters increase in length or complexity. We cannot itemise all the varieties but the following are worth looking out for. There are those which have a quite pronounced formal structure, with little digression, in which the subject is treated straightforwardly. *De l'amitié* (I, 28) subdivides into a discussion of relationships between father and

son, brothers, man and woman, husband and wife, homo-
sexuals, normal males and finally Montaigne and La Boétie.
Then there are the chapters which treat a central theme at greater
length than the earliest ones (I, 14, 20, 21, 25, 26; II, 8, 10, 16,
17, 37). By this time there are plenty of digressions from the
central theme, of course. Particularly worth noting are those,
including some quite early chapters, in which Montaigne
changes his original proposition in the course of the composition
(II, 2, 3, 11 for example).

Sayce (*1*, pp.265-79) has identified various other broad
categories: the binary form, in which two themes are presented
consecutively and may then oscillate (II, 2, 33; III, 10); ternary
form (II, 35, 36); direct entry, in which the opening immediately
deals with the subject announced in the title (III, 9, 13); indirect
entry, in which Montaigne approaches the subject in the title
obliquely (I, 9; II, 23); inverted order, in which the subject in the
title is reached only at the end (II, 18; III, 11, 12); chapters in
which there is a disparity between the title and the content (for
example, *Sur des vers de Virgile*, III, 5, seems to be mainly about
attitudes to sex, *Des coches*, III, 6, the New World and *Des
boyteux*, III, 10, witchcraft). The problem with all such
classifications, as Sayce recognises, is that they depend on
summaries of the subjects which cannot do justice to the
complexity of the original. The interweaving of the recurrent
themes complicates descriptions of this sort. When they occur
they can dominate the original line of development; equally,
they may flit in and out again very rapidly.

In the final analysis, most of the more complex chapters have
a form of their own which seems to grow organically rather than
to be imposed by the author. Such chapters, especially those in
Book III, have naturally fascinated critics; it is well worth while,
when tackling for example *De la vanité* (III, 9) or *Des coches*
(III, 6), looking at Sayce's structural analyses because he has the
space to illustrate in detail how the interpolations have a
beneficial effect by providing the links to 'attach themes to
themes and digressive movements to the central axis' (*1*, p.275).

Let us close this brief survey of a complicated area by
reminding ourselves that Montaigne himself provides the

justification for this sort of exploration. We have already seen
that he believes that all his ideas follow on naturally from what
precedes, but we must note that the link may not be obvious or
necessarily with what immediately precedes (III, 9, p.207B). He
is well aware of the rich diversity of material in the longer
chapters and that 'les noms de mes chapitres n'en embrassent
pas toujours la matiere'. He loves 'l'alleure poetique, à sauts et
gambades'; he makes it plain that in writing in this way he
knows the subject can be forgotten, the nub of the argument
discovered by chance and the development filled with extraneous
material. Even so, he never really loses sight of his subject
although an inattentive reader might. He shuns artificial
compartments: 'J'entends que la matiere se distingue soy-
mesmes. Elle montre assez où elle se change, où elle conclud'
(III, 9. p.208B).

Montaigne did not achieve the organic form of his chapters by
chance; his thoughts are not conveyed to us direct without the
intervention of art. They are transformed into patterns; the
sense of flow in an illusion created by aesthetic contrivance. We
can never know exactly how far Montaigne controlled the
process; we can be certain he was conscious of it.

Interacting with this process, however, is another, which is
apparently contradictory but in fact complementary. We have
already seen how Montaigne disliked rigid Ciceronian divisions
and subdivisions and thus adopted a more flexible, free-flowing
form of composition. We must now consider a further reason
why Montaigne cultivated an open form and a meandering style.
He was fully aware of the limitations of the intellect and the will
to control the human psyche, so he deliberately allows for the
effect of unconscious mental activity associated with the
memory.

Montaigne believed that both in the process whereby the
memory receives what it is supposed to store and in that whereby
it reproduces what it has already stored, conscious effort is only
partially effective. He notes that he has many good ideas 'à
l'improuveu et lors que je les cerche moins'. This is inconvenient
because they vanish before he can record them if he is on
horseback, at table or in bed (III, 5, p.91B). He knows that it is

just as impossible to make a conscious decision to remember
something as it is to forget; or rather, the decision is possible but
the effect is liable to be counter-productive: 'elle [= memoire]
me sert mieux par rencontre, il faut que je la sollicite
nonchalamment: car, si je la presse, elle s'estonne ... elle me sert
à son heure, non pas à la mienne' (II, 17, p.312A).

The importance of the link between what we may call the
involuntary memory and Montaigne's form and style is this. His
'dessein farouche et extravagant' makes extreme demands on the
resources of language. In a bid to overcome the limitations of a
linear verbal construction, Montaigne had recourse to numerous
devices to record the shifting patterns of human personality. He
had to give the impresssion of conveying the simultaneous
multiplicity of his being in a form which is logically limited to
chronological presentation. Montaigne's poor memory and the
impossibility of controlling its function was another potential
weakness. Even if his memory retained the essence of an
experience (and no conscious decision could ensure it would),
there was no certainty that any deliberate act would
subsequently permit him to recapture it. His knowledge of the
impotence of the will and his awareness that a chance
occurrence, an unexpected detail, an apparently irrelevant
digression might involuntarily lead him to a valuable discovery
about himself — all this must have had an influence on his
attitude to composition. Montaigne's meandering style may be
partly explained in terms of a search for those 'occasions
estrangeres et fortuites', those unexpected jogs to the memory
which would release experiences beyond the reach of conscious
recall. By writing without preordained categories and divisions,
Montaigne may have been trying to ensure the occurrence of as
many latent opportunities as he could for revealing those parts
of himself which might otherwise lie buried for ever in the
memory. 'Je ne me trouve pas où je me cherche; et me trouve
plus par rencontre que par l'inquisition de mon jugement' (I, 10,
p.78C).

Only a form as open as Montaigne could make it would create
the optimum conditions for the working of his involuntary
memory.

Style

Montaigne's comments on style abound and no single statement can be taken as definitive. In this, as in so many other areas, he elaborates details, elucidates ambiguities and modifies earlier opinions throughout the composition of the *Essais*. He often reminds us of the inseparability of style and content (III, 5, p.88B) yet he is quite capable of separating the two as well as, more significantly, allotting a different importance to each, even of expressing a preference for style rather than content (II, 10, p.78A; II, 8, p.142B). When we come to the more precise comments on the sort of style he admires, they almost invariably stress the qualities of directness, simplicity and freedom from literary artifice.

> Le parler que j'ayme, c'est un parler simple et naïf, tel sur le papier qu'à la bouche; un parler succulent et nerveux, court et serré, (C) non tant delicat et peigné comme vehement et brusque ... plustost difficile qu'ennuieux, esloingné d'affectation, desreglé, descousu et hardy; chaque lopin y face son corps; non pedantesque, non fratesque, non pleideresque, mais plustost soldatesque ...
> (I, 26, p.219A)

The conversational quality which is admired implies a need for swift communication without affectation. He approves of brevity, liveliness and muscularity of language because he fears to weary his reader; he prefers the forthright speech of the soldier to that of the scholar, the cleric or the lawyer, all of whom may use language to obscure their meaning or even the truth. His own style is that of the plain man, his 'langage n'a rien de facile et poly: il est aspre (C) et desdaigneux, (A) ayant ses dispositions libres et desreglées'. Yet even as he makes this claim he admits that 'à force de vouloir eviter l'art et l'affectation, j'y retombe d'une autre part' (II, 17, p.301A).

We should not allow ourselves to be misled by this talk of a direct, natural and unaffected style. Though some of what we have just seen of Montaigne's theory is, in fact, applicable to his practice, the *Essais* are full of rhetorical devices. He is a conscious and consummate stylist; he is critical only of those facets of rhetoric which would be contrary to his objectives in the *Essais*. Spontaneity is only one aspect of Montaigne's style; complementing it is the way in which he exploits all the hidden resources of language to manipulate the reader's response. This latter aspect of Montaigne's style has been admirably elucidated by McGowan (5, especially chapter 3 'Of the Craftie and Secrete Methode'). Why should Montaigne go to such lengths to conceal his art? First, it was common practice for sixteenth century writers to try to give the impression that their work was a trifle, dashed off effortlessly in haste. Second, Montaigne's occasional aristocratic pretensions gave him a particular reason to wish to differentiate himself from professional writers. Third, and perhaps most important, in presenting himself as a plain fellow he might more easily achieve that relationship with his reader by which he set so much store and, incidentally, allay that reader's suspicions about any disturbing ideas which he might express.

It would not be appropriate in a work of this sort to attempt anything like a full scale treatment of Montaigne's style. We shall try to indicate some of the more important recurrent features so that the reader has a number of pointers about the sort of examples to look out for. This is not entirely to make a virtue of necessity since it is preferable to become aware of stylistic features in the wider framework of seeking to interpret the meaning of the *Essais*.

Sentences

The next step down in dimension from the chapter might seem to be the paragraph. As we have already seen, Montaigne did not divide his work into paragraphs, presumably because he thought they might produce artificial divisions in the flow of his thoughts. We must even be cautious in considering the next unit, the sentence, because the punctuation of modern editions is not always reliable.

Montaigne's criticism of Cicero's general attitude to style is particularised in relation to sentence structure. In the lively

sixteenth-century debate on the relative merits of Cicero and
Seneca, Montaigne preferred 'une cadance qui tombe plus court,
coupée en yambes' (II, 10, p.86A), in the Senecan style, to the
sonorously balanced structures of the Ciceronian period.
Seneca's more informal structure in which ideas were only
loosely linked was more in keeping with Montaigne's
temperament than the highly mannered, tightly organised
Ciceronian period. In the following early example, the sentence
moves slowly forward, accumulating details in a series of
parentheses or juxtaposed clauses; the fragments are added as
the thoughts occur; the syntax is typical in that the present
participles gently ease the sentence onwards without the more
conspicuous *qui* or *que* which implies conscious, connective
links and subordination.

> Edouard premier, Roy d'Angleterre, ayant essayé aux
> longues guerres d'entre luy et Robert, Roy d'Escosse,
> combien sa presence donnoit d'advantage à ses affaires,
> rapportant tousjours la victoire de ce qu'il entreprenoit en
> personne, mourant, obligea son fils par solennel serment à
> ce qu'estant trespassé, il fist bouillir son corps pour
> desprendre sa chair d'avec les os, laquelle il fit enterrer; et
> quant aux os, qu'il les reservast pour les porter avec luy et
> en son armée, toutes les fois qu'il luy adviendroit d'avoir
> guerre contre les Escossais. (I, 3, pp.49-50A)

As Montaigne's experience developed, the long sentence
became the ideal vehicle not merely for anecdote or narrative,
but also for argument and exposition.

> Toute autre science est dommageable à celuy qui n'a la
> science de la bonté. Mais la raison que je cherchoys
> tantost, seroit-elle point aussi de là: que nostre estude en
> France n'ayant quasi autre but que le proufit, moins de
> ceux que nature a faict naistre à plus genereux offices que
> lucratifs, s'adonnant aux lettres, ou si courtement retirez,
> avant que d'en avoir prins le goût, à une profession qui
> n'a rien de commun aveq les livres, il ne reste plus

ordinairement, pour s'engager tout à faict à l'estude, que
les gens de basse fortune qui y questent des moyens à vivre.
(I, 25, p.188C)

The longer sentences appear at all stages of Montaigne's
composition, but side by side with them in B and C passages he
developed a complementary type which creates supple rhythms
and broken movements. Equally noteworthy and perhaps more
memorable are the aphorisms at the other end of the scale. Some
have a Senecan ring: 'Il est incertain où la mort nous attende,
attendons la partout' (I, 20, p.132A). Others are of a more
personal coinage: 'Il faut estre tousjours boté et prest à partir'
(I, 20, p.134A). He clearly cultivated the art of the telling
phrase. Consider this concrete summary of an abstract
discussion: 'Ferons nous à croire à nostre peau que les coups
d'estriviere la chatoüillent? Et à nostre goût que l'aloé soit du
vin de Graves?' (I, 14, p.96A). Or the controlled contempt of
'Après tout, c'est mettre ses conjectures à bien haut pris que
d'en faire cuire un homme tout vif' (III, 11, p.244B). Here
Montaigne's desire to communicate becomes an urgent need to
persuade and convince; as so often happens, the power of his
conviction of the truth as he sees it manifests itself in the
heightened language. The forcefulness of his conviction and of
his language are inseparable.

Images

This is a convenient place to touch on the way in which
Montaigne's images contribute to the sense of concreteness
which is such a prominent feature of his perception of the world.
Although, of course, similes do occur in the *Essais*, Montaigne
prefers to eliminate words like *comme* and *ainsi que* so that the
image and the reality are fused. This feature is most noticeable
in the fusion of the abstract with the concrete. The nature of
Montaigne's reflections and explorations leads him to use many
abstract terms ('vertu', 'ambition', 'honneur', 'inconstance' for
example). His great gift and strength is that he sees such
concepts always in practical terms and this characteristic mode

of thought is mirrored in a stylistic trait. He constantly combines
the abstract with the concrete in an illuminating image. He
draws his most typical and significant images from his everyday
life and experience. Moral and intellectual considerations are
infused with the physical; they are rooted in the language of the
familiar and the down-to-earth. One of the best examples is:
'Ma raison n'est pas duite à se courber et flechir, ce sont mes
genoux' (III, 8, p.150B), but once alerted the reader will find
countless others which stick in the mind.

The largest group of images in the *Essais* is concerned with
movement and change (which is hardly surprising since movement and change is one of the more important of the recurrent
themes). In such images Montaigne draws on various forms of
physical movement (for example walking, riding, hunting). 'Mes
conceptions et mon jugement ne marchent qu'à tastons,
chancelant, bronchant et chopant' (I, 26, p.194A). The two
largest groups deal with bodily sensations and the contrast
between *dedans* and *dehors*. For the former, Montaigne draws
on the ideas of food, hunger, illness and weight as well as the
relationship between his mind and physical functions.

> Le vice laisse, comme un ulcere en la chair, une repentance
> en l'ame, qui, tousjours s'egratigne et s'ensanglante elle
> mesme. Car la raison efface les autres tristesses et
> douleurs; mais elle engendre celle de la repentance, qui est
> plus griefve, d'autant qu'elle naist au dedans; comme le
> froid et le chaut des fiévres est plus poignant que celuy qui
> vient du dehors (III, 2, p.22B)

For the latter, there is some overlap with the former as the
quotation above illustrates; in addition, Montaigne uses the
ideas of acting, the face and the mask, the body and clothes, the
dyeing of material. 'La vertu ne veut estre suyvie que pour elle
mesme; et, si on emprunte par fois son masque pour autre
occasion, elle nous l'arrache aussi tost du visage' (II, 1, p.10A).
The smallest group and least personal are those which are
literary or visual.

The weakness of considering images in this classificatory
fashion is that it concentrates our attention too much on the

mere presence of an image, whereas we should be more concerned with its function. There is no single answer to the question 'What is the function of Montaigne's images?' First, he uses the common stock of conventional images (for example, the idea of nutrition and digestive processes as a model for a proper education in I, 25 and 26), but he often goes beyond this. Whereas conventional images may be used to obscure contentious or difficult points or act as comfortably recognisable guarantees of shared opinion, Montaigne often uses them to express his reservations about conventional opinions. As we have noticed, groups of Montaigne's images are inseparably interwoven with the central nexus of recurrent themes in the *Essais*. They are thus not only the expression of his constant preoccupations, they help to convey the sometimes irrational connections that Montaigne perceives between all branches of human activity.

In addition to the obvious pleasure that the images may give (in so far as this can be separated from their other functions), they also form a subtle part of that whole process whereby Montaigne aims to communicate his opinions and attitudes to the reader. When communication shades into a desire to convince the reader that what he is reading is worth taking seriously, Montaigne's images come into their own. We are not dealing here with a logical or coherent process of argument; reason gives way to an instinctive appreciation of Montaigne's perception of the relationships between all areas of human experience. His images convey his detachment, his lack of dogmatism, his viewing of problems from all angles; they inveigle the reader into considering the validity of ideas which reason or habit might lead him to discount. If reality is elusive, if nothing seems certain, how can plain verbal discourse impose order on the world without falsification? With images the effect does not depend on logic or coherence; they act more subtly, more insidiously and yet they find echoes in the disorder of our experience.[2]

[2] These conclusions owe a great deal to C. Clark's book, *The Web of Metaphor: studies in the imagery of Montaigne's Essais* (French Forum Monographs, Kentucky, 1978) which is the fullest and best treatment of Montaigne's imagery.

Words

In the consideration of individual words we may well ignore
Montaigne's own comments (I, 26, p.219A and II, 17, p.302A)
and criticisms in his own day about the number of Gasconisms
in the *Essais*. Modern research shows that criticism along these
lines is based on scant evidence. The English reader will find that
notes in modern editions will consign such examples as do occur
to a place of minor importance compared with the unfamiliar
archaisms of sixteenth-century vocabulary. Latinisms are
another matter. They are far more frequent, as is only to be
expected of a writer for whom Latin was for a time his native
tongue until it was supplanted by French (I, 26, p.221A). Yet
Montaigne was not of the generation which earlier, in an effort
to enrich the vernacular, deliberately sought to coin new words
in French based on Latin. Though he was certainly inventive in
his use of language in general, Montaigne both in principle and
in practice took a conservative attitude to neologisms (III, 5,
p.88B).

The range of Montaigne's vocabulary is wide; while it is most
often praised for being colloquial, racy, vivid and concrete, it is
also, by turns, erudite, abstract or technical (legal, medical or
military). More detailed study of Montaigne's style than is
appropriate here shows that even at the level of his use of
individual words, Montaigne is remarkable for his distinctly
personal touch. He is rarely content to follow the conventional
path. Whether it be in the use of noun or adjective, or his
particular favourites, the verb and adverb, he is constantly
striving for vigour, movement or concreteness by means of some
distinctive usage. Like many sixteenth-century writers he was
particularly partial to the doublet — a pair of adjective, adverbs
or verbs ('larmes... ou feintes ou peintes'; 'serieusement et
severement'; 'elle le ravist et ravage') with added alliteration in
these cases or with identical prefixes or suffixes ('me transporter
et transpercer') to stress the unity of the doublet. When the
doublet is lengthened into a triple or is transformed into an
enumeration, the effect is to suggest Montaigne's refusal of
simplification and the attempt to capture all the facets of the

topic under discussion. His indulgence in these stylistic features goes hand in hand with his wider use of puns, near puns ('tout ce qui plaist ne paist pas'), oxymoron, syllepsis and many other rhetorical devices. Their purpose is to please, to arrest, to involve the reader. An examination of Montaigne's additions and corrections shows clearly that these effects are consciously sought for.

Quotations

Quotations are a prominent feature of Montaigne's composition. One critic estimates 1,264 from Latin classics (*6*, p.82). In order to understand the part they play we must consider briefly the wider subject of Montaigne's reading.

What did Montaigne read? He claims he had a thousand volumes in his library; the roundness of the figure should inspire some caution but it is a huge number for the time. His acquaintance with the literature of the ancient world was impressive: he read Latin authors in the original, of course, while the Greeks were probably more often read in Latin or French translations although he did know some Greek. Among the authors he discussed and quoted most frequently were Seneca and Plutarch, Virgil and Plato, Cicero, Livy and Herodotus, Horace and Lucretius. There were many others, especially historians and poets, his two favourite types of writer, but those mentioned will be sufficient to indicate the quality of those who were important to him. By comparison, modern writers in Latin or French bulk much less large while the number of Christian works referred to is also limited (the Bible and St Augustine).

In the early stages of contact with Montaigne it is not the knowledge that he was influenced by this or that author that matters; one needs only to be aware that for Montaigne the ancient world was vibrantly alive. The characters and events he read about did not for him belong to a distant past; he speaks of them (Socrates in particular) as if they were still alive and the moral problems which confronted them are not merely bookish so far as Montaigne is concerned. They formed as valid an experience of life for him as contemporary events.

Admiration did not lead to adulation; the classics were read with a critical eye except that, when it suited him, Montaigne was apt to take anecdotes on trust (I, 21, pp.151-52A). He took from authors only what interested him; Plato was interesting because of the character of Socrates and the search for self-knowledge — the Platonic ideal and the rest of his immense work are largely ignored. When Montaigne quotes from an author he is quite capable, on occasion, of doing so out of context or inaccurately.

Montaigne's use of quotation reflects his own development. In the early stages, he was perhaps aware of the disproportion between his own inadequate attempts and the enormous stature of the classical authors. As a result, quotations were used to bolster his own hesitant opinions and remained inadequately integrated. As he realised the value of his own writing, quotations were more fully integrated, contrasting with or confirming his own contribution. Montaigne saw no contradiction in continuing his practice of using frequent quotations even when his objective was to make the *Essais* 'exactement mien' because he was confident that quotations (as well as translations, near translations and allusions), were all refracted through his own personality. For Montaigne, reading and experience were mutually enriching so that both had a beneficial effect on his means of self-expression.

Anecdotes

An obvious by-product of Montaigne's reading is the anecdotes which enrich the majority of his chapters. Varying in length from a sentence or two to well over a page, they may be merely the starting point of a chapter or embody its most important theme. Most are taken from Montaigne's wide reading of Latin historians, from contemporary moralists, from translations (notably from Amyot's sixteenth-century translation of Plutarch), from the stock of traditional folk tales and from his own experience. Where the source is written and identifiable, a great deal can be learned about his attitude to

composition by comparing his version with the original. Sometimes the imitation is very close, almost a translation; at others,
it is no more than a loose adaptation. Obviously during one's
early contacts with Montaigne, the *Essais* are far more
important than the sources, but it is very rewarding and
revealing to take the trouble to track down one or two examples
of near translation (of, say, Seneca in I, 20) and of free
adaptation in order to compare the *Essais* with some of the more
accessible sources, which are almost invariably indicated in the
notes of modern editions. Even if one's Latin is not too good,
one can get something out of the readily available translations.
Such a comparison shows how Montaigne eliminates or
compresses unnecessary detail, how he switches the emphasis
from, say, incident to emotion or from description to
characterisation. Or one can see how artfully he combines tones
which differ from those used in the original — third person
narrative with dialogues or first person interjections. In addition
to these personal touches, however, we find evidence that
Montaigne was an imitator working within a well-established
and honourable sixteenth-century tradition. In telling his
anecdotes, Montaigne could no more escape totally from this
tradition than he could escape from his legal or rhetorical
training: the telling phrase, the clinching argument, the balanced
antithesis, the relentless use of the same construction in
argument, the incisive question — all these bear the marks of the
court room and the college bench.

Another fruitful line of approach to Montaigne's style, which
we shall not pursue here, is to consider the variety and flexibility
in the tone and rhythm of his writing. Among the more obvious
examples worth looking out for are the conversational, the
consciously literary (even elegiac), the ironical, the paradoxical,
the humorous, the sententious, the assertive, the self-
deprecatory.

Montaigne needed to invent a method of composition, a form
of expression capable of giving the impression of transcending
the inherent weakness of words in capturing the shifting patterns
of human personality. We have seen in this chapter some

evidence of how, at every level of form and style, Montaigne
stretched traditional resources to the limit in an endlessly
ingenious and boldly innovatory effort to fashion a richly
textured artefact to convey his complex nature.

At the end of this short survey, let us remind ourselves of
Montaigne's view on the inseparability of form and content with
a final quotation: 'Je n'ay pas plus faict mon livre que mon livre
m'a faict, livre consubstantiel à son autheur, d'une occupation
propre, membre de ma vie' (II, 18, p.326C). As we pass from the
form to the ideas, we must bear in mind that this is only a critical
convenience, for they are different facets of the same thing.

5. *The Philosophical Background to the* Essais

Preliminary remarks

Before embarking on any closer examination of Montaigne's ideas we must first consider several underlying factors which will cloud the discussion if we do not deal with them straight away.

It is essential to remember that if we are to try to reshape the organic form of the *Essais* by compartmentalising Montaigne's ideas, we must be aware of the distortion we are perpetrating. If Montaigne had wanted his reader to be concerned primarily with abstracting his ideas from the *Essais* he would no doubt have said so (instead of insisting on the opposite) and he would have expounded them more systematically, eliminating the repetitions and the inconsistencies. Had he done this, the *Essais* would have turned out radically different. Always bearing this in mind, however, we do not need to deprive ourselves of the legitimate pleasure and, indeed, profit to be derived from observing such a fascinating mind play over so many fundamental, timeless questions which affect us all so deeply.

The purpose of the following remarks is two-fold. First, to alert the new reader to a set of factors which can cause difficulty in the study of ideas in the *Essais*. Second, to make clear from the outset that later indications about Montaigne's ideas should be treated as markers to be followed with caution rather than as summaries of all that it is essential to know.

It has already been suggested that even on a first reading a note should be kept of page references to major themes. This facilitates the assembling of widely scattered information. In reviewing the evidence on each topic, one often notices inconsistencies and even contradictions. Obviously some of these can be explained by changes in Montaigne's views over the years but this simple explanation is complicated by the fact that sometime C views are adumbrated in A passages while A views may be reinforced in C additions.

At this stage, the close study of the remaining inconsistencies reveals one of the most illuminating characteristics of Montaigne's writing. We earlier referred to the presence of the major recurring themes which represent the fundamental preoccupations of Montaigne's mind. By definition they reappear frequently, they interweave and they even seem to have a capacity for self-generation. More important, they can also lead Montaigne into inconsistency when he is carried away by his own argument at any particular moment. When these inconsistencies are examined, one is led to the conclusion that Montaigne sometimes expresses opinions which, it is legitimate to suppose from the weight of evidence elsewhere in the *Essais*, he did not really believe in, except at the moment of composition. Another way of putting this is to say that we should not always take what Montaigne says at its face value because of this process which might be called 'interference'.

Since this whole process seems to be at odds with the idea of perfect self-revelation, we had better pause to look in more detail. Montaigne himself admits, for example, that he is interested in ideas for their own sake: 'Maintes-fois (comme il m'advient de faire volontiers) ayant pris pour exercice et pour esbat à maintenir une contraire opinion à la mienne ...'; or he will arrogate other people's arguments and make them his own either because 'je ne trouve plus la raison de premier advis, et m'en despars' (II, 12, p.231B) or because he can think of arguments for both sides of the question ('ès choses humaines, à quelque bande qu'on panche, il se presente force apparences qui nous y confirment... de quelque costé que je me tourne, je me fournis toujours assez de cause et de vray-semblance pour m'y maintenir' (II, 17, p.316A)) and preferring not to remain in a state of doubt, he espouses the ideas of someone else who is surer of his ideas. Finally, he may advance quite seriously an argument which previously he had used only jokingly (III, 5, p.91B). Perhaps more common than any of these cases are those in which it is sufficient to consider the imperatives of the line of argument which Montaigne is pursuing within a given context to see how his normal attitude is modified to suit the case which he is arguing at the time. These are Montaigne's own words:

> Moy-mesme, qui faicts singuliere conscience de mentir...
> m'apperçoy toutesfois, aux propos que j'ay en main,
> qu'estant eschauffé (C) ou par la resistance d'un autre, ou
> par la propre chaleur de la narration, (B) je grossis et enfle
> mon subject par vois, mouvemens, vigueur et force de
> parolles, et encore par extension et amplification, non sans
> interest de la verité nayfve. (III, 11, p.239B)

So, in the context of conversation, Montaigne admits to being
carried away in the heat of the discussion, falling back on the
proviso in the next sentence that 'au premier qui me rameine et
qui me demande la verité nue et cruë, je quitte soudain mon
effort et la luy donne, sans exaggeration, sans emphase et
remplissage'. Who is to perform this task for the written word?
The answer is that it is a joint effort between Montaigne and the
reader but it can be a disconcerting process until one becomes
familiar with the *Essais*. Montaigne does provide sufficient
information somewhere for the reader to supply the corrective,
but not necessarily immediately after the departure from his true
opinion nor even in the same chapter. This process assumes
Montaigne is conscious of playing the devil's advocate or
pursuing a 'boutade'. Yet we have just seen that Montaigne
confesses he is not always in complete control and, in addition,
the process of interference is largely unconscious. The detection
of these passages is thus more difficult but when they are
identified they are very revealing. Experience can be acquired
more swiftly if one is alerted to these features from the outset.

It might be argued that inconsistency in Montaigne occurs
simply because he was inconsistent and he allowed the reader to
see this in the cause of self-revelation. There is a lot of truth in
this argument, of course, but it is weakened by the fact that
Montaigne sometimes deliberately masks facts which can only
be established from evidence outside the *Essais*. There are, for
example, the minor equivocations about the origins of the translation of Raimond Sebond's *Natural Theology* for his father,
about the length of time the family had resided at the château de
Montaigne or about La Boétie's age when he wrote his *Servitude*

Volontaire (I, 29, p.242A); there is evidence of doctoring the facts in his account of his brushes with some robbers in 1588. Then again, the typical process of composition by accretion is occasionally abandoned. Montaigne claimed that 'Je ne corrige point mes premieres imaginations par les secondes; (C) ouy à l'aventure quelque mot, mais pour diversifier, non pour oter' (II, 37, p.421A). Yet those who have made a special study of Montaigne's corrections have concluded that the alterations are not merely stylistic improvements of a trivial nature (removal of repeated or unnecessary words, for example); there are many cases in which the idea is changed and the original is removed. Finally, what becomes of self-revelation if, as Montaigne says, he has often changed what he wrote in the *Essais* in response to criticism of other people (III, 8, p.139C), or if he really thinks he can write exactly what he likes (without a thought for the reader), even if he does not necessarily believe it?

> Moy qui suis Roy de la matiere que je traicte, et qui n'en dois conte à personne, ne m'en crois pourtant pas du tout; je hasarde souvent des boutades de mon esprit, desquelles je me deffie, (C) et certaines finesses verbales, dequoy je secoue les oreilles; (B) mais je les laisse courir à l'avanture. (III, 8, p.158B)

There are a number of complicating factors, then, but having pointed them out, we must not exaggerate their importance. In practical terms, all that this implies is that we need to look especially carefully at what Montaigne says and, rather than simply take it at its face value, ask ourselves why he says what he does when he does and what importance he attached to it. Some of the suggestions just made may sometimes prove helpful when the obvious answers seem inappropriate.

The philosophical background to the Essais

Montaigne began to write his *Essais* over four hundred years ago. We all have to learn, sometimes painfully slowly, that enthusiasm and intelligence may not in themselves be enough to enable us to understand what the great writers of the past were trying to say. To understand what Montaigne meant we need to have some inkling of how he viewed the world. We may easily misinterpret what he says if we do not know what he assumes. The assumptions of a widely-read man of the Renaissance are not those of his twentieth-century counterpart. It is unlikely that the majority of the readers of these words will be soaked in the literature of the ancient world or familiar with the moral, philosophical or religious problems of sixteenth-century France. This is hardly anybody's fault but it is a fact that has to be recognised. The purpose of the section which follows is to provide the barest minimum of material to enable the reader to begin to appreciate the importance of some of the more unfamiliar concepts of Montaigne's period which impinge on his writing of the *Essais*.

Let us begin with the broad movement of humanism. Much ink has been spilled over definitions but, whichever way it is looked at, it has obvious importance for Montaigne's assumptions. If we think of the narrower end of the broad range of definitions and take the essence of humanism to be the study of the 'humanities' (*studia humanitatis*), there is an immediate link with Montaigne who is a prime example of a man steeped in a liberal, literary education based on a study of classical authors and concentrating especially on history, poetry and moral philosophy. He shared the humanist's scorn for the inelegance of the Latin of the medieval schoolmen and disliked their concentration on metaphysical speculation and logic chopping. If we move to the other end of the range we find humanism described as centrally concerned with the dignity of man. We might also note the stress on certain features which emphasise a reaction against the medieval world picture: for example, there is the concern with the concrete uniqueness of the feelings of the individual, the stress on the need for self-knowledge, the search for elegance, especially of language, and the repeated attempts to revive or absorb the teachings of the ancient philosophies. While the idea of the dignity of man needs to be treated with some care (because Montaigne, in the *Apologie*, destroys the

inflated idea of man propounded by some humanists) it is
plainly influential as we shall see in the final chapter; emphasis
on the individual in all his concrete and unique manifestations is
a central characteristic of Montaigne's perception. Like most
humanists he was acquainted with the ancient Greek schools of
philosophy. The three which are most directly relevant to
Montaigne are Stoicism, Scepticism and Epicureanism. The
interest of writers like Montaigne was concentrated on the moral
philosophies in particular. Ancient Greek attitudes to moral
problems pervade Montaigne's thinking; he transforms them
frequently but does not obscure them.

Stoicism

Stoicism was an ancient philosophy which had been
particularly relevant to a time in Greek history when the
individual needed to seek refuge in his own strength of character
because the world around him seemed to be crumbling
politically, morally and intellectually. A vogue of Stoicism
reached its peak in France around the time of the publication of
the *Essais*; it seemed to be tailor-made for a France racked by
civil wars which put the social and moral fabric under severe
strain at a time when, intellectually, the optimism of the early
humanists had turned to disillusion.

We shall concentrate first on those moral precepts of Stoicism
which influenced Montaigne and second on some aspects of the
metaphysical theory which will help to understand the rather
special meanings Montaigne sometimes gives to words like
'nature' and 'raison'.

The Stoic aims to control his passions to such an extent that
misfortunes such as illness, pain, poverty and death are seen as
matters of indifference. By unremitting effort and self-control,
the Stoic relies on his own resources since they are within his
control whereas the external world is not. The Stoic code is an
austere one; self-reliance can lead to pride.

In the Stoic system the whole of creation, often called
'nature', is permeated with the divine spirit of its creator. In
man this divine spirit is reason. The divine spirit shows a

preference for order which manifests itself in the form of fate. The aim of the Stoic is to use his reason to live in harmony with nature; virtue consists of living in harmony with nature and this is the only good. Man's freedom of choice within the confines of fate consists of accepting his fate or rejecting it. If he accepts it he will find happiness and live a life of virtue, for these two conditions are identical. All other considerations, pain or pleasure, self-preservation or death, are matters of indifference compared with the sole good which resides in virtue.

This barest of outlines should help us later to understand the context in which Montaigne used terms like 'suivre la nature' and 'la raison universelle'. We shall also see how Montaigne transforms the Stoic concepts and terminology into a peculiarly personal amalgam.

There is undoubtedly a strong Stoic influence in many of the chapters in Book I, especially those of the earliest period. Two of the more substantial chapters are among the best examples. The central argument of *Que philosopher, c'est apprendre à mourir* (I, 20) is that since death is certain and fear of death would ruin our whole life, we must face up to it resolutely and overcome its terrors by making it our constant preoccupation: 'aprenons à le soutenir de pied ferme, et à le combattre... Ostons luy l'estrangeté, pratiquons le, accoustumons le, n'ayons rien si souvent en la teste que la mort' (p.132A). The Stoic attitude to death is seen in a wider context in *Que le goust des biens et des maux depend en bonne partie de l'opinion que nous en avons* (I, 14), which examines the validity of the statement by the Stoic Epictetus, that we are more tormented by the idea that we have of things than we are by the things themselves. Death, poverty and pain are examined in turn and Montaigne concludes: 'Les choses ne sont pas si douloureuses, ny difficiles d'elles mesmes; mais nostre foiblesse et lascheté les fait telles' (p.108A).

In this next quotation we can see a number of typical Stoic elements: not merely detachment from life but almost a scorn for it together with a lofty sense of superiority and the crucial idea of dying nobly. 'Ce n'est pas grand chose que vivre; tes valets et les bestes vivent; mais c'est grand chose de mourir honnestement, sagement et constamment' (II, 13, p.273A). Montaigne's educational programme recommends that the child be taken away from its parents who would be inclined to be too soft. To prepare for life the child must grow accustomed to physical hardship, even pain, at an early age. Again, the pessimistic, defensive attitude to a hostile world is predominant: 'Il le faut rompre à la peine et aspreté des exercices, pour le dresser à la peine et aspreté de la desloueure, de la colique, du caustere, et de la geaule, et de la torture' (I, 26, p.201C). In the moral sphere, virtue can only be achieved as the result of over-coming difficulty by enormous effort of will; whatever is achieved easily is not virtue. 'La vertu refuse la facilité pour compaigne.... Elle demande un chemin aspre et espineux; elle veut avoir ou des difficultez estrangeres à luicter... ou des difficultez internes que luy apportent les appetits desordonnez et imperfections de nostre condition' (II, 11, p.92A). Finally, Montaigne's apparently callous attitude towards his wife and children may be seen, partly at least, as a Stoic attitude designed to ensure fuller control over his own happiness: 'Faisons que nostre contentement despende de nous; desprenons nous de toutes les liaisons qui nous attachent à autruy, gaignons sur nous de pouvoir à bon escient vivre seuls et y vivre à nostr'aise' (I, 39, p.292A).

Montaigne temperamentally disliked anything which impinged upon his ability to order his own life and to control his own peace of mind. The link with the Stoic code, based essentially on the individual's ability to remove the power of the external world to cause any pain and the search for a code whereby the individual achieves happiness from his own resources is very clear.

Stoicism became much less important for Montaigne after the early period of writing, even though it never entirely disappeared. In the *Apologie*, for example, Stoicism, along with other ancient philosophies, is the object of a fierce attack. In Book III Stoicism is not so much attacked directly as replaced by an alternative approach to life which contrasts strongly with the defensive bracing of the will inherent in Stoicism. Critics have often found it convenient to speak of three succeeding phases in the development of the *Essais*: the Stoic followed by the sceptical leading to the final phase, variously described as Epicurean or hedonistic. While this schematic division has some basis in fact, it is useful only if one remembers that it is a simplification which has to be further refined to take account of the whole, rather than of part, of the evidence. Chronological development is rarely sufficient to explain the complexity of Montaigne's views on most subjects; important though the time factor undoubtedly is, it explains only some of the evidence.

This is a principle of such importance for the understanding of the *Essais* that we must examine its implications in more detail without delay. A good example is Montaigne's treatment of the theme of death which we have already had to touch on. The chronological explanation of Montaigne's developing attitude to death might be summarised as follows: under the influence of Stoicism Montaigne recommends that one should steel oneself to the potentially disruptive fear of death by constantly keeping it to the forefront of the mind. In the later stages of his life, he thought that such efforts were unnecessary since Nature herself would play a vital role in preparing us for death, removing the element of fear by making us aware that it was no more than a normal part of the human process. 'A mon advis, c'est le vivre heureusement, non, comme disoit Antisthenes, le mourir heureusement qui faict l'humaine felicité' (III, 2, p.32C). For ease of reference let us call these Montaigne's A and C views while noting that they are virtually contradictory.

Bearing this in mind, we can see a number of fascinating features in the ostensibly Stoic chapter already referred to: *Que philosopher, c'est apprendre à mourir*. After restating his A view as 'le premediter donne sans doubte grand avantage', he almost immediately gives us, still in an A passage, the basis of his later C views in the following words, 'Nature mesme nous preste la main, et nous donne courage... à mesure que j'entre dans la maladie, j'entre naturellement en quelque desdein de la vie' (p.135-36A). A few pages later, after summing up various factors which make death seem less fearful, Montaigne comments: 'Voilà les bons advertissements de nostre mere nature' (p.141A). On several other occasions in this same chapter, we have a C view expressed in an A passage, but none captures the change from the Stoic view quite so well as the one in which Montaigne says he hopes 'que la mort me treuve plantant mes chous, mais *nonchalant* d'elle' (pp.134-35, my italics). The reverse process also occurs: typically A views are expressed in C additions, although one might explain these by saying that Montaigne is reinforcing at a later stage an idea to which he no longer subscribes (p.132C and p.135C).

All this, of course, is quite separate from the normal, later deliberate addition of C views to go side by side with A views. One way of interpreting this phenomenon is to say that the more extreme Stoic views were an example of Montaigne 'trying out' ideas which he did not necessarily totally believe in himself; the early appearance of the so-called later views would, on this interpretation, be expressions of his personal reactions to death bursting through in his writing to complicate his exposition of the bookish, second-hand Stoic philosophy.

To sum up, we might speak of a chronological development being much complicated by the early anticipation of later ideas and by the later echoing of apparently abandoned, earlier ideas.

We can find confirmation of this process in *De l'exercitation* (II, 6), which is probably a very early chapter. Montaigne recounts how he was thrown violently from his horse, and taken for dead for several hours; he himself recalls thinking he was dead. This personal experience convinces him that death need hold no terror; he describes his physical and mental condition during the time he thought he was dead as 'tres douce et paisible... c'estoit une langueur et une extreme foiblesse, sans aucune douleur' (p.47A). He draws the conclusion that 'pour s'aprivoiser à la mort, je trouve qu'il n'y a que de s'en avoisiner' (p.48A). Personal experience already counts for more than Stoic precepts.

Montaigne's temperament was such that he outgrew the restrictive influence of Stoicism as his awareness of the potentialities of life increased. By the time he came to write Book III, the following is more typical of his attitude: 'Qui ne peut atteindre à cette noble impassibilité Stoicque, qu'il se sauve au giron de cette mienne stupidité populaire. Ce que ceux-là faisoient par vertu, je me duits à le faire par complexion' (III, 10, p.232B). In more openly critical vein we read, '"Jettez vous en l'experience des maux qui vous peuvent arriver, nommément des plus extremes: esprouvez vous là, disent-ils, asseurez vous là." Au rebours, le plus facile et plus naturel seroit en descharger mesme sa pensée' (III, 12, p.261B). This does not mean that Stoic elements disappear entirely — indeed, they remain throughout the *Essais* — merely that they become subsumed in a more personal philosophy. The development of Montaigne's ideas on his favourite themes is rarely straight-forward and one must always be wary of chronological explanations.

Scepticism

Some time after his retirement Montaigne had over fifty maxims painted on the beams of his library. About a dozen were taken from Sextus Empiricus. What was Montaigne's interest in this classical philosopher who wrote around the end of the second century A.D.? Sextus was a sceptic, which means that he believed that no certain knowledge existed. His *Outlines of Pyrrhonism* was published in France in 1562. Pyrrhonism derives its name from Pyrrho of Elis, an early sceptic who predated Sextus by some hundred years. The distinction often drawn between a sceptic and a pyrrhonian is that the former claims we can be certain of nothing whereas the latter suspends judgement even on that. The following two maxims taken from Sextus's work by Montaigne sum up two of its central ideas: 'A tout raisonnement on peut opposer un raisonnement d'égale force'; 'Je suspends mon jugement'. The first expresses the book's fundamental principle and the second describes the sceptic's response which is based on the fact that we do not possess the means to decide between opposing propositions. Sextus advanced various arguments to support the second contention, including the variability of human judgements and customs as well as the fallibility of our senses. In order to make practical decisions which are necessary in everyday life, Sextus recommends following the customs and laws of one's own land; this, of course, does not imply that they have more validity than any others.

Sextus achieved enormous influence as a result of being rediscovered in the sixteenth century at a time when, after the Lutheran challenge to the Pope's authority, the difficulty of finding an alternative, acceptable criterion for the establishment of truth became a central feature of the intellectual debate stirred up by the Reformation.

Epistemological debates naturally have a long history. In the fourteenth century, William of Ockham had argued that it was impossible to prove the existence of God by human reason and had posited the separation of faith and reason, of theology and philosophy. The dominant, late medieval tradition, based on St Thomas Aquinas (c1225-74), had stressed the complementary relationship between faith and reason. Classical scepticism could be expected to arouse less opposition once the division between faith and reason was possible, because scepticism need not then lead inevitably to religious doubt. Erasmus used scepticism to undermine the religious dogmatism of the medieval, scholastic philosophers but reaffirmed faith based on a form of folly (another long tradition stretching as far back as Saint Paul), which was seen as superior to reason (*In Praise of Folly* (1509)). Even before the publication of Sextus's work in 1562, Gian Francesco Pico della Mirandola had been influenced by his writings and had attempted to discredit the rational, philosophical tradition of antiquity (*Examination of the Vanity of the Doctrine of the Pagans* (1520)). The purpose of his attack on reason was to enable him to show that man could find religious truth more certainly through revelation. Cornelius Agrippa in *On the Uncertainty and Vanity of the Sciences* (1526) ostensibly condemned all branches of knowledge in a long diatribe against intellectual activity. He urged that knowledge should be rejected in favour of simple belief stemming from God's revelation. Guy de Bruès published *Dialogues against the New Academics* (1558) which is concerned with the problems raised by scepticism while Sanchez in *Nothing is Known* (1581) concluded that by any

proper definition of the term knowledge is unattainable. These
matters can be pursued in the excellent short work by Burke (*6*,
pp.14-27) or at greater length in Popkin (*8*) and Busson (*10*).

In short then, though these brief descriptions cannot
adequately reflect the complexity of the issues involved, we can
at least see that two linked questions were being debated in the
works just referred to and, of course, more widely. First, the
problem of knowledge itself and, second, the impact of that
debate on theology. We will deal with the problem of knowledge
here and with religious matters in the next chapter.

What was Montaigne's attitude in this complicated area? We
can say for certain that whatever his attitude it was not
developed in isolation. He had read Sextus, Erasmus, Agrippa
and de Bruès and the reader of the *Essais* will find strong traces
of all the issues referred to above. We should first bear in mind
the distinction, made by Frame (*7*, p.52) between, on the one
hand, Montaigne's temperamental scepticism, a natural reaction
which colours his intellectual response to the variability and
uncertainty of life in all its manifestations and, on the other, the
conscious philosophical stance deliberately adopted because of
the impossibility of achieving certainty in the search for truth.

Montaigne's temperamental scepticism can be seen in his
comparatively early chapters, even before the very strong
influence of Sextus (c.1575-76) and the striking of the medal in
1576 bearing the motto 'Que sçay-je' on one side and a pair of
perfectly balanced scales on the other. It continues into the final
period also, although obviously it is more muted there. Let us
look at a few examples from the early chapters to get something
of the flavour. Various factors seem to Montaigne to come
between man and the truth. Imagination, for example,
constantly misleads the senses and distorts reality; Montaigne
illustrates this extensively in *De la force de l'imagination* (I, 21).
In one anecdote he tells of a woman who wrongly believed she
had swallowed a pin and who was only relieved of the pain she
actually felt when she was convinced that her vomit contained a
pin which had been surreptitiously placed there. In another he
tells of a man who, by way of a joke, announced a few days after
entertaining some guests that he had served them cat pie. As a

result a young lady contracted a violent stomach disorder and fever from which she died (I, 21, p.150A). The diversity of customs is catalogued at length in *De la coustume* (I, 23) and Montaigne remarks, 'l'usage nous desrobbe le vray visage des choses' (I, 23, p.163A). Perhaps more pervasive than these and other factors (such as chance and false learning), the major obstacle between man and truth is the changeability of human personality and thus of opinion and judgement. 'Certes, c'est un subject merveilleusement vain, divers et ondoyant que l'homme. Il est malaisé d'y fonder jugement constant et uniforme' (I, 1, p.41A). One final example from a chapter which, as one might guess from its title, contains countless similar comments: 'Nous sommes tous de lopins et d'une contexture informe et diverse, que chaque piece, chaque momant, faict son jeu. Et se trouve autant de difference de nous à nous mesmes, que de nous à autruy' (*De l'inconstance de nos actions*, II, 1, pp.10-11A).

The most systematic expression of Montaigne's philosophical scepticism comes in the *Apologie*. This complex essay will be dealt with more fully in the next chapter but it will be convenient to refer to the sceptical element briefly here. It contains not only a withering attack on the variability and unreliability of human reason and its judgements (II, 12, pp.227-30 for example) but also very powerful arguments to show why this is inevitable since all knowledge is based ultimately on our senses and these are manifestly fallible (II, 12, pp.253-57 for example). Montaigne is well aware of the far-reaching consequences of his argument which denies man the possibility of knowing anything for certain. 'Nous secouons icy les limites et dernieres clotures des sciences' (II, 12, p.223A; there are several similar comments on this on nearby pages). The only ancient philosophy which Montaigne sees as taking proper account of man's total incapacity for attaining truth is Pyrrhonism, whose position he describes as follows: 'Leurs façons de parler sont: Je n'establis rien; il n'est non plus ainsi qu'ainsin, ou que ny l'un ny l'autre: je ne le comprens point.... Leur effect, c'est une pure, entiere et tres-parfaicte surceance et suspension de jugement. Ils se servent de leur raison pour enquerir et pour debatre, mais non pas pour arrester et choisir' (II, 12, p.171A). Pyrrhonists in practical situations 'se prestent et accommodent aux inclinations naturelles... Ils laissent guider à ces choses là leurs actions communes, sans aucune opination ou jugement' (p.171A).

The *Apologie* deploys arguments which could have been found in Sextus, Agrippa, de Bruès and others; behind the *Apologie* lies a long tradition of ancient philosophy as well as Renaissance writing. One modern critic, R.H. Popkin, describes the *Apologie* as 'the *coup de grâce* to an entire intellectual world' and 'the womb of modern thought' (*8*, p.55).

This section of scepticism will leave a false impression if an antidote is not swiftly administered. Although Montaigne often speaks critically of reason, it is extremely important to draw distinctions between the sorts of reason he is talking about. This task is not made easier by the fact that he does not always make these distinctions himself. There is a difference between 'la raison universelle' and 'la raison humaine'. The former is viewed entirely favourably and corresponds to something like 'conscience'. Montaigne says he prefers the sort of virtue which is 'née en nous de ses propres racines par la semence de la raison universelle empreinte en tout homme non desnaturé' (III, 12, p.270-71C). This instinctive impulse towards what is good has some Christian overtones (such impulses are implanted by God (II, 12, p.207A)) but much more important are the powerful echoes of Stoic theory (each man is endowed with a divine spark and he should use this, his reason, to follow nature). This whole concept is intimately associated with beneficent Nature. We can see this link when Montaigne describes how some acts of wickedness arise because we have deliberately acted against 'les reigles de la raison, que nature a empreintes en nous' (I, 16, p.113A).

'La raison humaine', by contrast, is often subjected to attack, especially in the *Apologie*. 'J'appelle tousjours raison cette apparence de discours... c'est un instrument de plomb et de cire, alongeable, ployable et accommodable à tous biais et à toutes mesures' (II, 12, p.230A). There are countless similar passages in the *Apologie* but they are not found exclusively there (III, 11, p.238B). Human reason is most frequently criticised in contexts in which Montaigne judges that it is wrongly used. For example, in the *Apologie*, it is criticised because it has been used for pointless speculation in areas in which no certainty is attainable (metaphysical speculation about the nature of God, for instance). In *Des boyteux*, Montaigne's reluctance to believe in so-called miracles demonstrates his temperamental scepticism. The elaborate hoax perpetrated by a group of young people shows what happens when reason ('un instrument libre et vague') works on false premises unchecked by the senses; though they are often criticised in the *Apologie* and elsewhere, Montaigne realised the senses were the best checks we have. 'Les hommes, aux faicts qu'on leur propose, s'amusent plus volontiers à en cercher la raison qu'à en cercher la verité: ils laissent là les choses, et s'amusent à traiter les causes'. Instead of asking 'Comment est-ce que cela se faict?', they should ask 'Mais se fait-il?' Reason is 'capable d'estoffer cent autres mondes et d'en trouver les principes et la contexture. Il ne luy faut ny matiere, ny baze' (III, 11, p.238B).

In other contexts, Montaigne is quite capable of seeing that human reason is a tool which can be used for good or ill.

Oserons-nous donc dire que cet avantage de la raison... ait esté mis en nous pour nostre tourment?... L'intelligence qui nous a esté donnée pour nostre plus grand bien, l'employerons-nous à nostre ruine, combatans le dessein de nature et l'universel ordre des choses, qui porte que chacun use de ses utils et moyens pour sa commodité?' (I, 14, pp.95-96A)

The force of the context can work in the opposite direction: in *De l'affection des peres aux enfans*, Montaigne wants to reach the conclusion that books, the product of the mind, are much worthier progeny than our physical offspring, namely, our children. Here, unusually, he sets up an opposition between nature and reason and comes out very strongly in favour of reason. 'Nous devons bien prester un peu à la simple authorité de nature, mais non pas nous laisser tyranniquement emporter à elle; la seule raison doit avoir la conduite de nos inclinations' (II, 8, p.58A).

Montaigne's temperamental scepticism might seem to imply

that he would, at best, limit the role of reason to enquiry and debate without dogmatism. In fact, he went much further than this. He reserved a vital role for reason in the elaboration of his attitude to life in his final period. Reason was to play a crucial part in the greatest, practical task of all, the pursuit of happiness consistent with the basic nature of man. Without reason there could be no introspection, no fruitful observation of the raw material of observed experience, no transformation of knowledge into 'sagesse'. This will be more fully explored in the final chapter.

In the course of the *Essais* and particularly in the *Apologie*, Montaigne sometimes favours a non-thinking, non-rational approach to life. In arguing in favour of ignorance, he was echoing a long-standing tradition of primitivism. The praise of ignorance in the *Apologie* has to be seen in the context of a deliberate attempt to 'froisser et fouler aux pieds l'orgueil et humaine fiereté' (II, p.12, p.115A). Everything is thrown into the attack on 'la raison humaine' so that 'ignorance' becomes associated with countless, desirable qualities like 'innocence', 'humilité', 'crainte' and 'oḅéissance' (II, 12, p.164A), all of which, naturally, are conducive to uncritical religous faith. Yet even within the *Apologie*, when this contextual purpose is forgotten, Montaigne argues quite differently: 'Je suis content de n'estre pas malade; mais, si je le suis, je veux sçavoir que je le suis... qui desracineroit la cognoissance du mal, il extirperoit quand et quand la cognoissance de la volupté, et en fin aneantiroit l'homme' (II, 12, p.160C). The same oscillation attributable to the force of the context can be seen outside the *Apologie*, for example in *De la phisionomie*; having argued for moderation in everything, including learning, he quotes with approval some men who took a vow of ignorance. In a later addition he comments 'Et est richement accomplir le voeu de pauvreté, d'y joindre encore celle de l'esprit' (III, 12, p.250C). Montaigne's more normal attitude to ignorance, and the inevitable loss to the richness of life which ignorance would necessarily entail, comes out clearly in the following comment. 'La pauvreté des biens est aisé à guerir; la pauvreté de l'ame, impossible' (III, 10, p.221B).

Epicureanism

After considering the influence of Stoicism and Scepticism on Montaigne, we come now to Epicureanism which most affected his final period. Epicureanism was another of the Greek schools of philosophy which helped to shape the thought of the Renaissance. It was unique in being a full-blooded materialist philosophy: Epicureans maintain that the supreme good is pleasure and the supreme evil is pain. This hedonistic doctrine is easily misunderstood nowadays because of the debasement of the word Epicurean in modern parlance. Far from encouraging over-indulgence in those physical pleasures which are associated with pleasure, such as eating, drinking and making love, the true Epicurean, following Epicurus (341-270BC), is well aware that if pleasure is pursued without moderation, pain will ensue. Freedom from such pain must obviously enter into the calculation of how to pursue pleasure and thus moderation becomes a vital factor. Pleasures of the spirit, such as friendship or contemplation, may be equal or superior to physical pleasures. Man is freed from the fear of death itself and what follows because man is mortal and nothing exists for him thereafter. Fear of the supernatural is removed because natural causes and not the gods regulate the physical world. The pain of emotional turmoil can be avoided by keeping clear of immoderate emotional commitment. Thus, the torment sometimes associated with fear, ambition and jealousy for example, may be assuaged by means of a calculated approach to situations in which they might otherwise arise.

To the Christian, Epicureanism, particularly when transmitted through the works of Lucretius (94-55BC), was obviously an extremely dangerous doctrine since many of its central tenets (the cosmos is created by chance, man is exclusively mortal, there is no providential god, no reward or punishment in an after life) run counter to Christian doctrine.

Although we shall see in the next section that it is difficult to be certain whether Montaigne was influenced by the anti-religious element of Epicureanism, there can be no doubt that many of the other features just outlined can be found in the

Essais. The chapter dealing with Montaigne's final period will provide ample illustration.

Before leaving the ancient philosophies let us remind ourselves of the danger of too easily attaching labels to the phases of Montaigne's development. There were not three distinct phases — Stoic, Sceptical and Epicurean: these labels are useful only in that they denote tendencies which become temporarily more prominent than others. There are still traces of Stoicism in the later passages of Book III; Montaigne was always likely to show a sceptical turn of mind; the Epicureanism which predominates in Book III is adumbrated in the earliest Stoic chapters of Book I.

6. *Montaigne and Religion*

Of all the questions asked about the *Essais* none has produced such a wide variety of answers as 'What is Montaigne's attitude to religion?'. He has been seen as a blameless Catholic and Christian (albeit with some odd characteristics), as a good Catholic but a bad Christian, as a fideist of varying degrees, as a religious sceptic with a marked propensity for deception and as a thoroughgoing materialist beneath a prudently adopted mask of conformity. We must recognise at the outset that this question is too complex to attempt to resolve in a short work like this: the examination of the philosophical and theological background would take far too long. There is also the problem of attempting to interpret conflicting evidence when one cannot be certain whether orthodox expressions of belief are genuine or a cover for dangerous views which, if they are present, will naturally be conveyed indirectly to avoid the charge of heresy. All this is in addition to the usual problems we have discovered in establishing Montaigne's ideas.

All that the new reader should expect to do initially is to become conversant with the more accessible evidence and to take stock of the main interpretations which have been proposed. This chapter is meant to help readers to achieve these objectives. For reasons which I hope will become clear, the impossibility of giving a straight answer to the question 'What is Montaigne's attitude to religion?' need not undermine our overall approach to the understanding or appreciation of the *Essais*.

A fairly direct answer can be given to the more limited question 'What was Montaigne's religious practice?'. We know from the *Essais* that he himself prayed, having a predilection for the Lord's prayer; he recommended prayers at customary times during the day (on rising and retiring, at meal-times, etc.) and may well have based this on his own practice; he had strong views about trivialising prayer, and using God's name in everyday conversation without due reverence (*Des prières*, I, 56). Neither the *Essais* nor the *Journal de voyage* give a prominent place to Montaigne's attendance at mass, confession or communion but this can obviously be interpreted in different ways. Pilgrimages, the cult of saints and relics, much criticised by Protestants, were reaffirmed by the Council of Trent; Montaigne went on a pilgrimage, visited shrines and went to see relics during his foreign travels. In 1562, Montaigne made a formal declaration of his Catholic faith in Paris. When he died, full Catholic rites were observed at his request.

This evidence seems to indicate that Montaigne was a practising Catholic but it is inconclusive in relation to his religious views. Most of his behaviour in this respect is consistent with superficial, luke-warm conformity, although in the *Journal de voyage* there is perhaps evidence of curiosity and positive participation in religious affairs beyond the needs of outward conformity. More important, scrupulous observance of traditional religious forms is in line with the Pyrrhonistic position: religion is a public, political necessity, as well as a non-committal deference to custom; scepticism is a private affair, for the philosopher not the masses. When Montaigne argues in favour of religion as a bulwark of the political, social and legal system (I, 23, p.167B for example), he may be doing no more than echoing free-thinkers who believed that state religion was necessary to keep most people more or less moral.

Passing from Montaigne's religious practice to his attitudes, we shall look first at the *Apologie* and then at the evidence in the rest of the *Essais*.

The 'Apologie de Raimond Sebond'

Many of the difficulties of describing Montaigne's religious attitude stem from the apparently contradictory nature of the *Apologie*. The circumstances in which Montaigne wrote it are a matter of conjecture but they are probably a useful key to understanding Montaigne's longest and, in many ways, most famous chapter.

Like most of the longer chapters in the 1580 edition, the

Apologie was not written in one go; unlike the other chapters, however, this one is probably made up of rather long sections, written at different times and for a rather different purpose from the one to which they were eventually put. Large sections dealing with human presumption were probably written in 1573 for a chapter on that subject. Another section dealing with man's ignorance and praising the Pyrrhonians was probably written in 1576, again as the basis of a general chapter on this general theme. The most likely explanation of how the *Apologie* came to be put together is as follows. Marguerite de Valois, the Catholic wife of Henri de Navarre, asked Montaigne to write a defence of Raimond de Sebond's *Natural Theology* which she had been reading in Montaigne's translation. In 1578-79, when she joined her husband in Gascony, she may have been anxious to combat the arguments of the Protestants around her. For various reasons (especially the fact that he did not share Sebond's view about the importance of reason in religious matters), Montaigne felt embarrassed by the request but obliged to respond positively, in spite of feeling no particular competence in such matters. Thus, in 1579, he wrote a brief introduction dealing with the two objections which critics had made of Sebond and cobbled this (and possibly some additional passages) together with the mass of material written earlier in 1573 and 1576. A fuller account can be found in Frame's biography (*3*, pp.171-73).

So the *Apologie* was probably composed, initially at least, out of duty not pleasure. Its massive length may be due to the unusual circumstances described above. The internal inconsistencies may be attributable, in part, to the patch-work nature of the composition. More significant, however, is the fact that Montaigne's habit of pursuing the rhetorical tradition of arguing a point he does not necessarily fully believe in (which we have commented on before) is present here on the grand scale as arguments are piled one upon the other.

The *Apologie* seems much less puzzling if we abandon the idea that it was a single, cohesive unit specifically written with a straightforward objective. It will be useful to try to get an overall view of its constituent parts.

(1) There is an introduction which discusses how Montaigne came to translate Sebond's work (pp.105-06; probably written in 1579).

(2) Montaigne then defends Sebond against the attack on the principle of using reason to bolster faith. Montaigne accepts the pre-eminence of faith but argues that it is permissible to use reason (one of God's gifts) when it is illuminated by faith (pp.107-15, 1579).

(3) Montaigne passes to the second defence against the criticism that Sebond's arguments are weak. His method is to 'froisser et fouler aux pieds l'orgueil et humaine fierté' (pp.115-19, 1579). The first part of this consists of a section in which Montaigne argues that animals are in many ways, including intellectually, man's equal or superior (pp.119-52, probably written in 1573). Where man is endowed with supposedly superior faculties (such as imagination) they do not make him happier or more virtuous.

The second section is a long attack on knowledge and a praise of ignorance (pp.152-222, mostly written in 1576). Montaigne maintains that knowledge has no practical value (for health, for example), does not necessarily lead to virtue, and is dangerous for religious faith. Ignorance, on the other hand, is our natural state, is conducive to the cure of pain and illness and is a firm basis for faith (pp.155-67). Ancient philosophies are arraigned except for Pyrrhonism (pp.168-72). The weakness of human reason to comprehend God (pp.178-82), or man himself (important sections on 'ame' and immortality pp.207-221) is contemptuously documented. These ideas (and others) are sometimes intermingled.

(4) Montaigne warns the noble lady to be satisfied with the preceding arguments in defending Sebond. He, however, will continue with a 'dernier tour d'escrime' (p.223), which consists of an attack on the basis of all human knowledge (pp.223-67, 1576 or 1579?). Man is by nature ignorant of fundamental causes, he is constantly in a state of flux, he cannot know the essence of things because his knowledge is based on the senses which are manifestly liable to error, being influenced by the passions and his physical disposition. Man may even be lacking

some vital faculty without being aware of it (pp.227 and 252-57).

(5) The conclusion contrasts the uncertainty and the inconstancy of man with the certitude and immutability of God. Montaigne concludes that man can only raise himself above his inherent feebleness 'si Dieu lui preste extraordinairement la main' (p.268).

The *Apologie*, which purports to defend Sebond's concept of a theology based on reason, does so only briefly and concentrates longer and more powerful sections on the undermining of human reason. Sebond's hierarchy of nature with man at the summit because of the power of reason is shown to be a monstrous presumption.

The crucial question about the *Apologie* is whether it is the work of a genuine believer or that of a sceptical non-believer. The opening sections contain many religious comments which are apparently straightforwardly in line with the avowed purpose of the chapter. A great deal of the closing pages, apparently unambiguously, contrasts the certitude and immutability of God with the uncertainty and transience of man. In following the text of the chapter with the help of the plan the reader will find a number of orthodox Christian comments made unambiguously and with reverence. There are passages in which a distinction is drawn between Christian and pagan virtues to the advantage of the former. The 'actions vertueuses' of Cato and Socrates 'demeurent vaines et inutiles' because they were ignorant of God (p.114A); in spite of his many great qualities, Plato likewise is to be judged merely on the human scale because he was ignorant of 'nostre sainte verité' (p.113B). If all such passages are taken as premeditated precautions against persecution then Montaigne is guilty of deception which, however comprehensible, runs completely counter to his repeated and passionate outbursts against hypocrisy.

On the other hand, even if it is argued that the long section devoted to philosophical scepticism is not necessarily anti-religious because the concept of scepticism as a tool was familiar to sixteenth-century Catholic fideists, there remains a great deal

of evidence which casts doubts on an orthodox religious interpretation. There is the pervading ambiguity of so many
arguments (even in the opening and closing sections referred to
earlier) and the frequent criticism of features of other religions
or philosophies which suggest obvious parallels with Christianity
(see for example p.197 and p.239). The series of comments
about the soul and immortality allows Montaigne to make
indirectly critical, even derogatory, remarks about the nature of
the after-life, and why people must believe in it, which spill
over on to the orthodox position. Lucretius, whose godless
philosophy was so un-Christian, is quoted in this connection and
many others, some seventy times in the *Apologie*. Though
humanists often happily import classical authors into Christian
contexts, this is hardly an adequate explanation in the *Apologie*.
There is also the problem of explaining the fulsome praise of the
moral qualities of the Brazilians who are 'sans relligion quel-
conque' (p.158).

One could, perhaps, conclude that the *Apologie* is incapable
of being interpreted coherently since the evidence is inherently
contradictory. The question then arises whether this is an
accident which stems from the circumstances surrounding its
composition or whether it is by design. If it is by design this
might simply be the result of Montaigne's customary attitude to
inconsistency or it might be that he deliberately leaves us in
doubt or makes interpretation impossible. The ending may well
be an example of the latter explanation because, in a section
which he rewrote several times, Montaigne describes the
essential Christian concept that man can only transcend his
essential weakness 'si Dieu lui preste extraordinairement la
main' (p.268) as both 'absurde' and 'miraculeuse'. Both
adjectives are in C passages and seem deliberately paradoxical;
they can be interpreted either in an orthodox religious way (God
can achieve the 'absurde' by his 'miraculeuse' powers) or as
implying that the idea of a miracle is absurd.

Most critics believe that some of the difficulties of
interpretation are removed if the *Apologie* is seen firmly in the
context of fideism. The disadvantage with such an explanation is
that fideism, the abandoning of reason as a means of

apprehending religious truth, can be adopted both by genuine
Christians and by those who seek only a cover to permit their
rational criticism of certain aspects of Christianity while
maintaining, dishonestly, that this does not affect their religious
faith. Fideism would thus allow one to interpret the chapter as
the work of an orthodox Catholic who entertained many
dangerous, sceptical ideas but not seriously enough for his
genuine faith to be affected. Alternatively, large parts of the
Apologie might be explained by the fideist distinction, but with
quite different implications. If the gift of faith is withheld, one
inevitably remains a sceptic; it may be true that not to have faith
does not prevent one from conforming to religious practices but
this practice is obviously inferior to true faith. If this is how the
fideist position in the *Apologie* is to be interpreted, it has to be
taken in conjunction with the evidence in the rest of the *Essais*.
If, in the *Essais* as a whole, it were then found that Montaigne
showed no signs of having any religious beliefs other than the
sort that he had dismissed as inferior in the *Apologie*, the
conclusion which the reader would have to draw on the basis of
these two propositions is that Montaigne was a religious sceptic.
On this interpretation, Montaigne would expect some alert
readers at least to reach this conclusion which he could never
dare to express explicitly.

What can we learn about Montaigne's attitude to religion if
we leave the narrow context of the argument in the *Apologie*?
We shall have to limit ourselves to some brief comments on a
number of important elements which new readers will want to
keep in mind while compiling their own list of relevant evidence.

First a brief general remark. It is to prejudge the issue to
assume that Montaigne's many protestations about his
ignorance in theological matters are an attempt to avoid
suspicion. When he apologises in advance for any expression of
opinion which contravenes 'les sainctes prescriptions de l'Eglise
catholique, apostolique et Romaine, en laquelle je meurs et en
laquelle je suis nay' (I, 56, p.377C; see also II, 3, p.21A), we
might take this as no more than an extension of his usual non-
specialist attitude to all the subjects he treats in the *Essais* or no

more than a genuinely prudent precaution in view of his propensity to play with ideas or, indeed, be carried away by them. Or Montaigne might be covering up dangerous religious views. This may be true about all orthodox religious comments that Montaigne makes. Some have argued that he gives the reader a strong hint when he says the *Essais* contain 'la semence d'une matiere plus riche et hardie' not only 'pour moy qui n'en veux exprimer davantage' but also 'pour ceux qui rencontreront mon air' (I, 40, p.303C). When seen fully in context this, and other similar expressions (III, 9, p.209C for example), can be perfectly well explained in terms of the complex task of self-revelation without the need to think of self-protection.

To begin with the positive religious comments, Montaigne speaks out forcibly against those whose supposed faith is not reflected in their everyday actions; this is the burden of much of the early section of the *Apologie*.

> Si ce rayon de la divinité nous touchait aucunement, il y paroistroit par tout; non seulement nos parolles, mais encore nos operations en porteroient la lueur et le lustre. Tout ce qui partiroit de nous, on le verroit illuminé de cette noble clarté. (II, 12, p.108A; also p.110 and p.112)

This seems unambiguous yet, as so often, one cannot be sure if the 'nous' really includes Montaigne himself.

Montaigne makes many positive references to the existence of God (see for example, I, 32, pp.265-66A; I, 56, p.378A; II, 12, pp.165, 178-82, 189-92, 242). For Montaigne, God seems essentially unapproachable and incomprehensible (except when He is virtually indistinguishable from Nature as we shall see in the next chapter). References to God's grace are not always wrapped up in the ambiguities of the *Apologie* (for example, I, 56, p.381C; III, 1, p.15C; III, 10, p.236B) while the discussion in *Des prières* (I, 56) is set in a reverential Christian context.

Montaigne's attitude, especially his Catholicism, can also be approached by examining his comments on Protestantism. In interpreting this part of the evidence, we must remember that his critical comments will be coloured by his hatred of cruelty, his general suspicion of change and his belief in the need for a 'police ecclesiastique' to preserve a certain level of moral behaviour.

Montaigne condemned believers in 'la Religion pretendue reformée' (II, 32, p.382A) for their arrogance in wishing to over-throw established religion, thus causing untold civil strife, on the strength of their own 'privée fantasie' (I, 23, pp.167-68). He argued against vernacular translations of the Bible, maintaining that 'le Sainct livre des sacrez mysteres' was best interpreted by those who had devoted their lives to it. He viewed with alarm the idea of each individual having a personal relationship with God or challenging the 'prescriptions et formules de la foy establies par les anciens' (I, 56, pp.380-81). Protestants were criticised for introducing that canker of doubt which, for the mass of people, could so easily lead to atheism, which he denounces in traditional terms (II, 12, p.106A and p.112C). He believed that any concession to the Protestants on matters of doctrine would be dangerous and wrong; it would encourage further demands and the authority of the Church should not be questioned (I, 27, p.230A). Any departure from 'la voye tracée et battuë par l'Eglise' (II, 12, p.186A) was liable to lead to disaster. Montaigne particularly feared that the masses might be persuaded that 'la religieuse creance... seule et sans les mœurs' was sufficient to 'contenter la divine justice' (III, 12, p.271C).

Montaigne, of course, saw the strengths and weaknesses of both Catholics and Protestants (III, 10, pp.224-25). In particular he knew both were guilty of using religious strife to pursue political and personal objectives and that even when the motives were exclusively religious, intolerance and fanaticism were to be found on both sides (II, 19, 330A).

At one point, in a way which is quite out of keeping with his normal position, Montaigne says that it is difficult to know whether the religious wars are on balance more useful than harmful ('je ne sçay si l'utilité ne surmonte point le dommage' (II, 15, p.279A)). The wars are described as an act of Divine Providence which has given renewed vigour and strength to inactive Catholics and this is seen as outweighing the defections. Interference is surely at work here: Montaigne makes this point about the religious wars because it fits in with the burden of much of what precedes in the chapter, that is, the beneficial effects of opposition.

Apart from the *Apologie*, the majority of the *Essais* are concerned with non-religious matters dealt with, for the most part, in a non-religious way. Montaigne apologises for his 'fantasies humaines et miennes' which he claims are expressed essentially in a manner which is 'laïque, non clericale, mais très-religieuse tousjours' (I, 56, p.383C).[3] Although humanists commonly mingle the classical and the Biblical, we are forcibly struck by the massive number of classical references compared with the few dozen from the Bible. Montaigne's sources, quotations, examples and opinions are predominantly non-religious. He has very little that is specific to say about the great doctrinal issues.

If one examines his treatment of such subjects as miracles, immortality and witches one finds his position is ambiguous or untypical of an orthodox believer. For example, the conventional Catholic view of miracles was that they represented God's intervention in the laws of nature and the suspension of their normal course. Montaigne says a number of different things: to reject miracles is an example of human presumption in limiting God's power (II, 30, p.374C); that what we call miracles might well be explicable according to the laws of nature if only we were more knowledgeable (I, 23, p.158C and I, 27, pp.227-28A); that so-called miracles are in fact the result of the immense power of human imagination (I, 21, p.145A); that miracles are the result of the embellishment of a story in transmission (III, 11, p.239B).

---

[3] This factor, like much of the evidence in this chapter, can be interpreted in a completely different way. For example, in a recent study by M. Smith entitled *Montaigne and the Roman Censors* (Droz, Geneva, 1981), the author argues that because Montaigne is concerned with 'tests or trials', his book is 'human' rather than 'theological' (p.73). This explains the relative absence of religious pronouncements, which, in any case, Montaigne would have thought improper from a Catholic layman. He also maintains (1) that *Du repentir* has a strong Catholic substructure (pp.67-68); (2) that *De l'experience* shows 'the authoritative voice of nature behind whom Montaigne discerns the guiding hand of the Creator' (p.110); (3) that Montaigne more than once 'adopts the language of a "confession" in a religious sense' (p.71); and (4) that the later *Essais* contain 'more and more professions of indebtedness to the Creator, professions which are progressively more committed and authoritarian in tone' (p.112).

Montaigne's comments on immortality range from the positive statement that it is God's great gift to us which ensures 'la jouyssance de la beatitude eternelle' (II, 12, p.219A) to the opposite negative extreme: 'Ce qui a cessé une fois d'estre, n'est plus' (II, 12, p.185A). It is true that the second comment refers narrowly to metempsychosis but this is a good illustration of the way in which Montaigne's comments about other philosophies and religions could easily be transferred to Christianity. When, for example, he links Plato's vision of the after-life with Mahommed's promise of a paradise full of gold and precious stones, 'peuplé de garses d'excellente beauté, de vins et de vivres singuliers', his conclusion that 'ce sont des moqueurs' (II, 12, p.183A) could easily be applied by the reader to Christianity. The later Montaigne's comments are, on both miracles and immortality, the more difficult it generally is to reconcile them with orthodox opinion.

Montaigne's views on witches, too, are far from conventional. Writing at a time when witch-burning was reaching a climax, he does not seem to share the general view that they were possessed by the devil and represented a serious threat to good Christians. After personally questioning a group of people accused of witch-craft he concluded that they needed an antidote to cure their madness rather than to be put to death (III, 11, p.244B). Montaigne's mistrust of the supernatural, his abhorrence of cruelty or fanaticism and his tolerance in a period in which this was seen as a weakness, mark him out from his religious contemporaries.

Perhaps more significant than any of these individual soundings is the absence of any all-pervading, deeply felt conviction of the exclusive truth of Christianity. Whatever religious beliefs Montaigne may have had, they did not lead to the guiding principles which underpinned his everyday thoughts, words and deeds. These seem to be clearly non-religious. Even when Montaigne deals with subjects which might be thought to have obvious religious implications, these turn out to be slight or absent. There are many examples of this (education, suicide, death) but particularly telling is the almost total absence of any religious dimension in a late chapter devoted to the idea of repentance (*Du repentir*, II, 2).

Another example, even more significant, is the fact that in the chapter in which Montaigne sums up his attitude to life (*De l'experience*, III, 13), the predominant tone is hardly Christian; it is far more often pagan and hedonistic. Where God does briefly appear in the final pages, He is referred to respectfully as someone who has imposed upon man the task of maximising his human potential ('nous en devons conte jusques à un poil' p.326B). When Montaigne says, 'Pour moy donc, j'ayme la vie et la cultive telle qu'il a pleu à Dieu nous l'octroier' (p.324C), he suggests that God's role ends with the granting ('octroier') of life and the setting of limits to human potential (implied in 'telle que'). Man's task begins then and the chapter as a whole concentrates on how much Montaigne relishes and cultivates ('ayme' and 'cultive') this precious gift of life. Whereas one might have expected this final testament to bear witness to man's helplessness without the transforming power of God's grace, Montaigne concentrates on the human dimension, on the need to accept the limits on the human condition and the need to strive to achieve one's full potential here and now by human means alone. Socrates rather than Christ is held up as a model of human behaviour, and even he is criticised for those aspects of his life which were not essentially human ('ses ecstases et ses demoneries' p.327C). Montaigne chose to close his whole work with an apostrophe to a pagan god, Apollo, by a pagan poet, Horace, in which the emphasis is on life and health, pleasure and contentment.

7. *Some Key Ideas in the* Essais

The evidence of the *Essais* leads us to conclude that, whatever the truth about Montaigne's religious beliefs, they did not permeate his ideas sufficiently for us constantly to be aware of them recurring in his description of his everyday life and thoughts. What, then are the key ideas which permeate his thought? In trying to give an account of some of the most important and most typical we shall largely concentrate on that final phase of Montaigne's writing which saw the flowering of his control over his form and the increase of his confidence in the value, to himself and to others, of the twin processes of self-study and self-revelation.

We begin with the idea of nature. The word itself and its derivatives occur with great frequency; Montaigne uses it in so many different and overlapping ways that we cannot here attempt to catalogue them all. We will concentrate instead on Montaigne's attitude to the potent complex of ideas which he evokes by his use of the word. With occasional exceptions, Montaigne's attitude is one of almost unbounded approval and trust and we should try to explain why.

First, we have already seen the idea of order which permeates the Stoic concept of nature when this denotes the whole physical universe ('nostre mere nature en son entiere magesté' (I, 26, p.205A)). Part of Montaigne sought for certainty amid the continual flux of life and perhaps he felt he might find it in nature's predetermined order. Nature and God are sometimes used almost interchangeably so that there is an overlap, if not an identity, of meaning (III, 6, p.115B and III, 13, pp.324-25). In expressions such as 'Nature peut tout et fait tout' (I, 25, p.189C), nature seems to acquire the characteristics of God. Second, custom, habit and tradition are conventionally described by Montaigne as a 'seconde nature' (III, 10, p.222B); when he recommends them as a means of determining behaviour

in the absence of any surer criterion, this is a further example of
seeking a refuge from uncertainty. Probably more important
than either of these two explanations (associated with two of the
less frequently occurring meanings of nature in the *Essais*), is the
fact that the most common single idea that Montaigne associates
with the word is 'intrinsic' or 'essential'. He speaks of 'Le travail
et le plaisir' as being 'très-dissemblables de nature' (II, 20,
p.334C); in the context of people, he relates how Plato's rule
was to ensure that citizens were given 'selon leur nature, leur
charge' (I, 25, p.189C). By extension and dilution the meaning
sometimes becomes 'original' or 'first'; speaking of his opinions
Montaigne says he has hardly 'alteré les miennes premieres et
naturelles' (II, 12, p.235A). Montaigne eventually came to
believe that the only firm basis for establishing a way of life was
in self-knowledge; it is thus the individual essence which
becomes the objective of the search described in the final phases
of the *Essais*. The word which encapsulated the essence of such
an important theme in the *Essais* would obviously acquire a
powerful favourable charge. This usage is frequently very
difficult to separate from another which was useful for
expressing some of Montaigne's favourite ideas. In the sixteenth
century, nature was often defined by contrasting it with art.
Thus, what is instinctive is preferred to what is acquired, what is
simple is superior to what is complicated. In a comment such as
'Ce n'est pas raison que l'art gaigne le point d'honneur sur
nostre grande et puissante mere nature' (I, 31, p.254A) we see
how the notion of 'bonté naturelle' in unsophisticated man
(cannibals, in fact) is connected with more than one meaning of
this complex word. Animals too have the advantage that
'nature, par une douceur maternelle, les accompaigne et guide,
comme par la main, à toutes les actions et commoditez de leur
vie' (II, 12, p.122A). The nature/art opposition was closely
connected in Montaigne's mind with the whole objective of
perfect self-revelation in his writing and this in its turn was
linked with the nature/essence concept. When this potent
combination was reinforced by the other favourable
connotations already noted, it seems to have produced a
complex but powerful nexus of loosely associated ideas which

Montaigne referred to frequently and with great confidence.

Within this area of ideas covered by 'nature' is the more limited concept of 'bien né' which is vital to a proper understanding of Montaigne's ideas, especially in the areas of good and evil, vice and virtue.[4] We can best begin by allowing Montaigne to express the tone of his confidence in this aspect of human make-up.

> Il n'est vice veritablement vice qui n'offence... à l'advanture ceux-là ont raison qui disent qu'il est principalement produict par bestise et ignorance. Tant est-il malaisé d'imaginer qu'on le cognoisse sans le haïr... Il n'est, pareillement, bonté qui ne resjouysse une nature bien née. (III, 2, p.22B)

This brings out very well the optimism inherent in Montaigne's attitude. Those who are fortunate enough to be 'bien nés' have within them an instinctive inclination towards what is good, an impulse to do what is virtuous. Conversely, they need merely to see vice to eschew it. To see the right path is also to take it, for not to take it implies an inability to see it rather than a rejection of it. Knowledge and morality are assimilated, thus confirming the most fundamental precept of Montaigne's views on education in *Du pedantisme* and *De l'institution des enfans*: 'Il falloit s'enquerir qui est mieux sçavant, non qui est plus sçavant' (I, 25, p.184A) and 'Le guain de nostre estude, c'est en estre devenu meilleur et plus sage' (I, 26, p.200C).

The second aspect of 'bien né' shown in the quotation is that virtue is its own reward; such people behave virtuously by instinct and they derive pleasure from so behaving. These ideas were first formulated by the Stoics, so this is another reason to beware of simple notions about Montaigne abandoning Stoicism. 'Bien né' in Montaigne, and generally in the sixteenth century, has nothing to do with social class or high birth

---

[4] There is a fuller treatment of the idea of 'bien né' in my article 'Montaigne and the concept of 'bien né'', *Bibliothèque d'humanisme et Renaissance*, 30 (1968) 483-98. The origins and history of the term, as well as its use in the sixteenth century, have been illuminated by S.M. Gauna, 'Fruitful fields and blessed spirits', *Etudes rabelaisiennes*, 15 (1980), 117-28. His article is also very pertinent to Montaigne because of its comments on Stoicism.

(although a class connotation — even a financial one — does once become added to the moral core as a later quotation will show). It is a moral description which implies an inherent predisposition to love what is good.

There is a darker side to this concept. If you are not 'bien né', there is not much hope for you.

> J'essayeroy, par une douce conversation, de nourrir en mes enfans une vive amitié et bienveillance non feinte en mon endroict, ce qu'on gaigne aiséement en une nature bien née; car si ce sont bestes furieuses... il les faut hayr et fuyr pour telles. (II, 8, p.64A)

To be 'bien né' provides a sufficient basis for subsequent favourable development through education and environment but if a child does not respond to the sort of treatment Montaigne favours (constantly qualified as 'naturel'), then, he concludes: 'je n'y trouve autre remede, sinon que de bonne heure son gouverneur l'estrangle, s'il est sans tesmoins, ou qu'on le mette patissier dans quelque bonne ville, fust-il fils d'un duc...' (I, 26, p.210C). The tone is humorous on the surface but the implications are clear. Although the moral impulse to do good can be developed and refined in the 'bien nés' there is little that can be done with those who are not. Montaigne's generally favourable attitude to nature should not lead us to assume that most people, or indeed many people were 'bien nés'. Perhaps not surprisingly Montaigne does not often touch on this pessimistic side of things but when he does he says that such people 'sont bien rares' (III, 8, p.146B).

Montaigne's concern over the implications of this form of fatalism may colour his ambivalent treatment of the question of whether or not it is possible to change one's basic nature. Even in *Du repentir*, where this general concept is most pronounced, Montaigne seems reluctant to accept that some people (who are 'collez au vice d'une attache naturelle' and who constantly commit 'pechez de complexion' (III, 2, p.28B)) cannot rectify the flaw inherent in their nature.

The generally favourable attitude to the 'bien nés' can be

further examined in a narrower area which is of central importance for Montaigne's final period. In *Du pedantisme*, Montaigne confronts the problem of why pedants are unable to use their often considerable knowledge to become better men. Their memories are stuffed full, but their judgement and understanding are underdeveloped. The chapter is packed with examples of their inability to make use of their learning; they are unable to transform intellectual knowledge into practical wisdom. Montaigne describes knowledge as 'un dangereux glaive, et qui empesche et offence son maistre, s'il est en main foible, et qui n'en sçache l'usage' (I, 25, p.188A). The reason why they are unable to make use of their learning is made explicit: '... de ces gens là [= pedants] les ames, estant et par nature et par domestique institution et example du plus bas aloy, rapportent faucement le fruit de la science' (I, 25, p.189A). They cannot handle the 'dangereux glaive' because they are not 'bien nés' and here, unusually, there does seem to be a social as well as a moral connotation because, in the previous sentence, such people have been described as 'gens de basse fortune qui y questent des moyens à vivre'. Not only does 'science' have to be put to use since it is only a tool, but it can only be used properly by certain people. 'Science' can do nothing where 'nature' has not already predisposed favourably. These views underlie much of Montaigne's writing but they are rarely seen as clearly as in the following passages from *De l'art de conferer*:

C'est chose [= sçavoir] de qualité à peu près indifférente; très-utile accessoire à une ame bien née, pernicieux à une autre ame et dommageable. (III, 8, p.142B)

C'est chose de grand poix que la science; ils [= tant d'ineptes ames] fondent dessoubs. Pour estaller et distribuer cette noble et puissante matiere, pour l'employer et s'en ayder, leur engin n'a ny assez de vigueur, ny assez de maniement: elle ne peut qu'en une forte nature; or elles sont bien rares... (C) Elle paroist et inutile et vicieuse quand elle est mal estuyée. (III, 8, p.146B)

The pessimistic side of the argument is very pronounced here; in the wrong hands knowledge is not merely useless, it is positively dangerous. The Stoic echoes are again very strong.

These preliminary considerations enable us to see the link between 'science', which may be used for good or ill and 'raison' which we saw earlier was, likewise, capable of being put to good or bad uses. Montaigne's mistrust of formal logic and pure reason (see for example I, 26, p.209A; II, 10, p.84A; III, 8, p.209A; III, 13, p.280B) is not so much forgotten as pushed from the foreground in the final phase when he concentrates on showing how man's cognitive faculties (referred to by a range of terms including 'jugement', 'entendement', 'discours' and 'raison') can be used positively to bring about the new objectives in life which stand out clearly in any close examination of the writings of this period.

'Experience', which is the subject of the final chapter becomes a key concept. The word, in Montaigne, is used in a number of ways. First, to refer to a single act or event; secondly, to refer to the total of those single acts or events stored in 'le magasin de la memoire' (I, 9, p.72B); third, in the sense of the 'fruit of experience', where this phrase refers to the benefits which accrue when experience as defined under the second meaning is properly used. We can see something of these distinctions in the following quotation:

> Quel que soit donq le fruict que nous pouvons avoir de
> l'experience, à peine servira beaucoup à nostre institution
> celle que nous tirons des exemples estrangers, si nous
> faisons si mal nostre proffict de celle que nous avons de
> nous mesme.' (III, 13, p.283B)

When Montaigne at the beginning of *De l'experience* opposes reason to experience as different ways of approaching knowledge or truth, he describes experience as being 'un moyen plus foible et moins digne'. This has surprised some commentators because, in many ways, the chapter is a monument to the fundamental role of experience in Montaigne's final period. It is less surprising, however, if the reason which he refers to in this chapter is taken to mean reason used in a way of which Montaigne would have approved. We recall that his attitude varies according to the use to which reason is put. The crucial feature about the final phase is the way in which Montaigne envisages that the mind (our cognitive faculties) should interact with experience. Experience is not useful in itself, it needs to be used. One can profit from experience only if one knows how to draw the proper conclusions and this does not happen automatically. The immense value of experience is that it provides the raw material on which the mind can work. When this interaction functions properly the dangers of theorizing in a void are circumvented. This is why the relationship is one of the corner-stones of one of Montaigne's favourite notions, the inseparability of body and mind ('corps et ame'). Metaphysical systems and formal logic are rejected; reason is brought to bear on the data provided by our everyday experience which is essentially rooted in direct contacts through physical sensations. We can see how Montaigne perceives the interaction in the following formulation: 'De l'experience que j'ay de moy, je trouve assez dequoy me faire sage, si j'estoy bon escholier' (III, 13, p.284B). We notice that the objective is wisdom. What Montaigne means by wisdom is what we must now try to illustrate. Let us take as a starting point a revealing quotation:

> Je leur dirois volontiers que le fruict de l'experience d'un chirurgien n'est pas l'histoire de ses practiques, et se souvenir qu'il a guery quatre empestez et trois gouteux, s'il ne sçait de cet usage tirer dequoy former son jugement...
> Ce n'est pas assez de compter les experiences, il les faut poiser et assortir et les faut avoir digerées et alambiquées, pour en tirer les raisons et conclusions qu'elles portent. (III, 8, pp.145-46B)

We can see reiterated here the interaction between mind and experience, but there is a new factor. Whereas before we saw that the objective was wisdom, here Montaigne expresses the result in a slightly different way. 'Jugement' is what results when 'experience' is distilled and for Montaigne it is the key faculty in dealing with the problems of living; 'son institution, son travail et estude ne vise qu'à le former' (I, 26, p.199A). This early formulation in Book I contains many of the essential mature features even though the context of a child's education might be thought to limit the scope of the discussion. The essence of the method is that the student's 'jugement' is formed by direct confrontation with the problems of living: the world is his text-book. 'Il se tire une merveilleuse clarté, pour le jugement humain, de la frequentation du monde... Ce grand monde... je veux que ce soit le livre de mon escholier' (p.205A). The student will develop acute powers of self-criticism and will learn how to be wise and good before he tackles academic subjects. In dealing with education Montaigne always distinguishes between the moral and the intellectual sphere; characteristically, he puts the moral sphere first in both time and value.

One of the fundamental characteristics of Montaigne's mature approach to life is that, being rooted in experience, it is essentially practical. This shows itself in many ways. For example, Montaigne refuses to concern himself with the unknowable or the unchangeable; he looks at the human condition and takes it as his starting point. Refusing externally imposed moral codes, partly on principle (because they are not personal), partly because they may prove to be inappropriate, Montaigne recognises after his long process of introspection that he has the strengths and weaknesses of a man. The pattern of his life which he must work out for himself must be appropriate to a man, not to an angel nor a horse: '... ma conscience se contente de soy, non comme de la conscience d'un ange ou d'un cheval mais comme de la conscience d'un homme' (III, 2, p.22C). Montaigne's inner serenity would be constantly disturbed if he were to set himself standards attainable only by an angel and then constantly to fall short. Yet he would not be true to the proper dignity of man's condition if he were to set his sights too low.

Acceptance of the human condition also implies acceptance of the fact that man consists of both body and mind, as we noted briefly earlier in a different context. They are not warring factions, there is little point in deciding which is the more important, they are equally important and, in fact, indissoluble. If we recognise this and pay equal attention to each we shall be likely to achieve greater satisfaction.

> A quoy faire desmembrons nous en divorce un bastiment tissu d'une si joincte et fraternelle correspondance? Au rebours, renouons le par mutuels offices. Que l'esprit esveille et vivifie la pesanteur du corps, le corps arreste la legereté de l'esprit et la fixe. (III, 13, p.326B)

The acceptance of the harmony of body and mind soon leads to positive pleasures and this adds a new dimension to the final phase. It is worth noting that the rejection of dualism is specifically Epicurean and that when the meaning of 'ame' is 'soul' rather than or as well as 'mind' (oscillation and overlap are frequent in the *Essais*), it is un-Christian as well. Life is not merely something to be got through, it is something from which the maximum of pleasure should be extracted by using all the faculties which are part of our make-up. The interplay of mind and body is here seen in a slightly different light: some people are negligent in the way they treat their lives; some of them

> ne pensent point avoir meilleur compte de leur vie que de la couler et eschapper, de la passer, gauchir et, autant qu'il est en eux, ignorer et fuir, comme chose de qualité ennuyeuse et desdaignable. Mais je la cognois autre, et la trouve et prisable et commode, voyre en son dernier decours, où je la tiens... Il y a du mesnage à la jouyr; je la jouys au double des autres, car la mesure en la jouyssance depend du plus ou moins d'application que nous y prestons. (III, 13, p.323B)

Montaigne pours fierce scorn on those who despise physical pleasures because no intellectual effort is required. He wonders why such people do not give up breathing. In any case, the simplest of physical activities are enhanced when the intellectual faculties participate simultaneously. Montaigne describes this reciprocal action in the beautiful chiasmus 'intellectuellement

sensibles, sensiblement intellectuels' (III, 13, p.319C). The
pleasures of each and every moment are precious: whether you
are walking in an orchard, dancing or sleeping, you should strive
to savour it with all your faculties.

Through this approach to life, Montaigne suggests an
unfamiliar scale of values. Even the most apparently trivial
events in the daily round are not to be disdained, indeed they are
more important than writing books, winning battles, ruling
countries, amassing fortunes and building monuments which are
exceptional, directed towards other people and may be merely
for show.

> Composer nos meurs est nostre office, non pas composer
> des livres, et gaigner, non pas des batailles et provinces,
> mais l'ordre et tranquillité à nostre conduite. Nostre grand
> et glorieux chef-d'œuvre, c'est vivre à propos. Toutes
> autres choses, regner, thesaurier, bastir, n'en sont
> qu'appendicules et adminicules pour le plus. (III, 13,
> p.320C)

This implies that moral decisions are not rejected but are worked
out personally rather than imposed from without. The supreme
dignity of life is reflected in the phrase 'grand et glorieux chef
d'œuvre' while some of the essential objectives of the moral
decision are indicated by the words 'ordre' and 'tranquillité'. As
Montaigne himself puts it so elegantly and directly, it is not
important to show what you can do in exceptional cirumstances,
you need only know how to 'mediter et manier vostre vie' for if
you can do that 'vous avez faict la plus grande besoigne de
toutes' (p.320C).

The pursuit of pleasure, however, which we saw referred to
above, is not unbridled. As a true Epicurean, Montaigne
recommends moderation lest the pleasure be diminished in itself
or involve unfortunate after-effects:

> Il ne faut pas se precipiter si eperduement après nos
> affections et interests. Comme, estant jeune, je
> m'opposois au progrez de l'amour que je sentoy trop

> avancer sur moy, et estudiois qu'il ne me fut si aggreable
> qu'il vint à me forcer en fin et captiver du tout à sa mercy,
> j'en use de mesme à toutes autres occasions où ma volonté
> se prend avec trop d'appetit. (III, 10, p.226B)

The revised hierarchy of the important events in life and the
inseparability of body and mind form part of a wider area of
Montaigne's investigation. He made a number of profound
observations as a result of what we should today call his psychological approach. For example, the interaction of body and
mind meant a need to abandon any clear distinction between
physical and mental reactions. What Montaigne observes is
simply a wide range of phenomena, some of which are conscious
and some of which seem simply to be unconscious reflexes. The
subconscious is for Montaigne a tantalizing and uncharted
region in the search for self-knowledge.

In the process of recording the variability of his own
personality ('l'instabilité de ma posture' (II, 1, p.8B)) and trying
to establish his motivation, Montaigne came to an important
conclusion. This was that beneath the surface changes of human
personality there exists a fundamental, immutable bed-rock
which forms the core of a person's make-up. He called it the
'forme-maistresse'.

> Regardez un peu comment s'en porte nostre experience: il
> n'est personne, s'il s'escoute, qui ne descouvre en soy une
> forme sienne, une forme maistresse, qui luicte contre
> l'institution, et contre la tempeste des passions qui luy sont
> contraires. (III, 2, p.26B)

A major feature of the difficult process of introspection is that it
allows one to identify the nature of this 'forme-maistresse'
which forms part of our psychological sub-strata. Since it is by
definition unalterable ('on n'extirpe pas ces qualitez originelles'
(p.26B)), it is essential to construct a code of behaviour which
does not conflict with one's inherent propensities. If one does
not do this it will be impossible to achieve the sense of inward
peace and serenity which Montaigne considers so essential.

Montaigne's conclusion was that, difficult though it may be to discern through the constantly changing pattern, there is a 'forme-maistresse' of both body and mind. This explains why such large sections of the chapter *De l'experience* are devoted to Montaigne's physical condition, to doctors and to health as well as to superficially trivial accounts of his preferences and intimate habits such as eating, drinking, sleeping, love-making, dressing, washing. They all help Montaigne to build up a picture of his physical 'forme-maistresse'. As he says: 'J'ay assez vescu, pour mettre en compte l'usage qui m'a conduict si loing... Ma santé, c'est maintenir sans destourbier mon estat accoustumé' (III, 13, p.290B). He knows from experience better than any doctor what is likely to do him good when his body is disturbed. One of the reasons why Montaigne so disliked doctors (like pedants they are his *bêtes noires*) was that they behaved as if medicine was a discipline like logic; they failed to check their premises against the evidence of their senses. Unchecked reason thus led at best to no improvement in the patient or at worst to death (II, 37, pp.426-38).

Genuine introspection is difficult because it involves the breaking down of *idées reçues* and predetermined categories. Another aspect of Montaigne's revision of the normal scale of values is his recognition that behind great events lies a conglomeration of tiny incidents. Our minds seize upon and become preoccupied with trivial events: 'Nous ne regardons gueres les subjects en gros et seuls; ce sont des circonstances ou des images menues ou superficieles qui nous frapent' (III, 4, 52B). We may be steadfast in facing death in the abstract, but when confronted with the practical details, 'les larmes d'un laquais, la dispensation de ma desferre, l'attouchement d'une main connue' (III, 4, p.53C), we may be inconsolable. Montaigne seized upon these qualities which were inherent in the human mind and combining them with another, our constant wish to escape from the present ('nous pensons tousjours ailleurs'), he proposed the notion of 'diversion'. At its simplest, this is an oblique way of finding consolation in adversity; at a more profound level it is a general principle to replace Stoic fortitude.

On the basis of the psychological data provided by his introspection Montaigne constructs an individual code of morality
from which external constraints are largely excluded: custom
and habit are guidelines for matters not of particular concern to
the individual conscience. In discussing the abstract concept of
virtue, Montaigne first distinguishes between 'vertu' which
'presuppose de la difficulté et du contraste' (II, 11, p.91A) and
'bonté' which is natural and easy for those who are 'bien nés',
but then realises that the weakness of this distinction is that it
would exclude Socrates from the ranks of the virtuous since his
conduct betrayed no trace of difficulty or effort. Montaigne
rapidly reformulates his views and proposes a three level
hierarchy which allows Socrates a position at the top. The
greatest virtue is one which, though effort is involved at an early
phase, is performed without any difficulty because people in this
category have 'une si parfaicte habitude à la vertu qu'elle leur est
passée en complexion' (II, 11, p.95A). At the second level are
those who struggle to achieve virtue while the third (including
Montaigne) contains those fortunate enough to be born with a
nature which is 'dégoustée par soy mesme de la débauche et du
vice' (p.95A). The discussion is a good example of Montaigne
'trying out' his ideas rather than simply recording his
conclusions. In the final phase, the concept of difficulty is left
even further behind; in the context of a gentle hedonism, 'la
vertu est qualité plaisante et gaye' (III, 5, p.60B). His confidence
in 'nature' allows Montaigne to describe virtue as having its own
reward as we have already seen (III, 2, p.22B). Specific examples
of the sort of virtue which Montaigne most admires deal with
personal relationships and he transfers to these the prestige
normally accorded to public acts.

> Gaigner une bresche, conduire une ambassade, regir un
> peuple, ce sont actions esclatantes. Tancer, rire, vendre,
> payer, aymer, hayr et converser avec les siens et avec
> soymesme doucement et justement, ne relácher point, ne se
> desmentir point, c'est chose plus rare, plus difficile et
> moins remarquable. (III, 2, p.24-25B)

'Gloire' is rejected while the need for consistency of performance reminds us that in making moral judgements we must consider 'l'homme tout entier' (II, 11, p.96A).

It would be wrong to leave the impression that, because Montaigne is primarily concerned with his own behaviour, he believed he had no obligation towards others. Even in the early chapter *De la solitude* (I, 39) Montaigne writes fascinatingly on this subject. After his retirement from his magistracy, the motives for which were complex, he might appear to be extremely egotistic in his search for tranquillity and peace of mind free from obligations: 'La plus grande chose du monde, c'est de sçavoir estre à soy' (p.293A). Montaigne may even have been anticipating criticism when he supports his decision to retire by quoting from ancient authors, by stressing the corruption of public life in the sixteenth century and by indicating that he was temperamentally unsuited to it. The egotism is somewhat softened if we remember that his attitude is part of a Stoic defensiveness, part of his desire always to be in control over whatever affects his personal happiness: 'il faut avoir femmes, enfans, biens, et sur tout de la santé, qui peut; mais non pas s'y attacher en maniere que nostre heur en despende' (p.292A). Even in the early phase 'la vraie solitude' is a frame of mind and can be found 'au milieu des villes et des cours des Roys' (p.291A); the real key to freedom is to be found in self-knowledge and self-control: 'Retirez-vous en vous, mais preparez vous premierement de vous y recevoir; ce seroit folie de vous fier à vous mesmes, si vous ne vous sçavez gouverner' (p.299A).

Montaigne's reflections on his experience as mayor of Bordeaux give a focus to his earlier generalisations when he provides his major formulation of his views on commitment in *De mesnager sa volonté* (III, 10). It is plain that he has thought the problem through. Though a man's primary obligation is to himself, this cannot be fully satisfied without the realisation that 'il doibt appliquer à soy l'usage des autres hommes et du monde, et, pour ce faire, contribuer à la société publique les devoirs et offices qui le touchent' (III, 10, p.219B). This sort of

enlightened self-interest is more strongly expressed in the C
addition: 'Qui ne vit aucunement à autruy, ne vit guere à soy'.
Provided that the obligations are 'par emprunt et accidentale-
ment' so that the mind can always remain 'en repos et en santé'
(p.219B), so that, unlike his father, he can remain untouched by
the 'agitation intestine' of the 'tracasserie publique', Montaigne
is prepared to involve himself. Even though, as Montaigne's
famous formula has it, 'le Maire et Montaigne ont tousjours esté
deux, d'une separation bien claire' (p.224B), it is apparent that
his style of involvement, in practice has many advantages. Not
only did Montaigne act 'fidelement et conscientieusement', but
he performed more effectively because he never allowed himself
to be controlled by the job. Moreover, he was astute enough to
realise that, in principle, involvement meant becoming mixed up
with 'la fourbe', with 'vice' and with 'sottise'. He claimed that
his detachment enabled him to detect the faults in his own
actions and in those of his own side while at the same time
recognizing what was admirable in the opposition (p.224).

Given the sixteenth-century context, it was inevitable that
Montaigne's political thinking should have been deeply
influenced by the religious wars. Much of his condemnation of
the Protestants stemmed from his observation of the fact that
their desire for change had plunged France into a state of chaos
in which the political, social and moral fabric was badly
damaged. Montaigne's dislike of change was pragmatic as well
as temperamental. He believed that no political system could be
so bad that it was worth risking changing it; that it would be
impossible to change part of any system without destroying the
whole of it; that blue-prints for improvement could never be
implemented because of existing habits and customs and that
men are always liable to thwart them because of their inherent
human weaknesses (I, 23, pp.165-66; II, 17, p.318A; III, 9,
pp.169-70).

If the rejection of change seems at odds with the simultaneous
postulation of the universal law of movement and change (III, 2,
p.20B), this is only superficially so. Just as amid the flux of
human personality Montaigne sought for the certainty of the
'forme-maistresse', so in the wider context of the external world

it was logical for him to seek for elements of permanence by preserving those over which we have some control. Montaigne offered no systematic political theory, of course, but he was acquainted (III, 7, p.133B) with the two conventional sixteenth-century explanations for the basis for the king's power: viz, that either it derives from God and is thus absolute or from the people and is therefore limited. The consequence of this latter explanation is that rebellion against the king may in some circumstances be justified and some Protestants obviously exploited this possibility. It was a highly contentious issue and both Catholics and Protestants changed their positions on this when it suited them in the civil wars. Montaigne thought that the monarchy was best for France because it was a system which the country was used to (III, 9, p.70B); no principle was involved, merely the belief that different systems are appropriate to different societies because of their habits and traditions. His loyalty was to the crown rather than to the individual and did not preclude independence of judgement (III, 8, p.150B). He thought general rules had little relevance to human affairs; different courses could lead to identical results while identical courses could equally lead to different results (I, 1). However, though Montaigne may recommend that whatever is traditional and stable is better than what is new and untried, he does not want anyone to be under any illusions about why change is undesirable. The parallels between politics and law are very strong. Where kings and judges are concerned Montaigne distinguishes sharply between the mask and the man, between the magnificent apparel and the pomp associated with the office and the human weakness inherent in the fallible man beneath (III, 10, p.223B). There are no absolutes in politics or the law; no general formulation in either sphere can match the complexity and changeability of human custom and behaviour; laws are 'fixes et immobiles' while our actions are 'en perpetuelle mutation'. Thus, in his famous formulation 'Or les loix se maintiennent en credit, non par ce qu'elles sont justes, mais par ce qu'elles sont loix. C'est le fondement mystique de leur authorité; elles n'en ont poinct d'autre' (III, 13, p.283B), Montaigne strips away all illusion with an uncomfortable directness. His conclusions reinforce traditional forms; unlike those of most sixteenth-century thinkers, his reasons are his own and make no appeal to tradition.

When we examined Montaigne's attitude towards himself we noted a dominant strain of individualism and independence. The counterpart of this in his way of thinking about the external world is his stress on the rights of others. The rejection of compulsion or constraint on himself is equally applicable where others are concerned. Whereas many in the sixteenth century felt threatened by differences in other people (it was an important factor in the religious wars), Montaigne counted many Protestants among his friends.

Montaigne's unorthodoxy can be seen clearly in his attitude to two specific cases. He hated cruelty: 'Je hay, entre autres vices, cruellement la cruauté, et par nature et par jugement, comme l'extreme de tous les vices' (II, 11, p.98A). It is perhaps difficult for us today to appreciate Montaigne's unorthodoxy in this matter. The cruelty inherent in sixteenth-century attitudes to judicial torture, either as a deterrent or as a means of procuring a confession was not merely a fact of life, it was the orthodox position. Montaigne rejected it not only because of his finely tuned sensitivity to the feelings of others (II, 11, p.99A), nor even solely on the grounds that it could not logically achieve the desired effect (II, 5, p.39A; II, 27, p.361A), but also because of his attitude to the dignity of life and because of his feeling towards his fellow men.

The second example is Montaigne's treatment of colonialism. Beyond the more often noted fact that Montaigne presents the natives of South America as examples of natural goodness and a contrast to the moral and physical corruption of Europeans, he also goes much further. In *Des coches*, after countless examples of exploitation of the natives by the Spanish invaders, he can hardly contain his anger at the senseless torture and killing of individuals or of a group of four hundred and sixty people. All this is not the inevitable accompaniment of war, it is merely to capture slaves or to acquire 'la doubteuse information de quelque vase d'or à piller' (III, 6, p.128B). Montaigne's

imagination is heightened by the intensity of his feelings and he
imagines what might have been if some ancient leader like
Alexander had led the conquest. He would have been able to
infuse the noble virtues of the ancient world into the natural
qualities of the natives, thus making it easy to establish 'entre
eux et nous une fraternele societé et intelligence' (III, 6, p.125B).
There is no condescension here, only fraternal feeling of a sort
which was rare in the sixteenth century.

Conclusion

In essence, the central quest of the *Essais* is a search for self-identity whose objective is to reveal how life should be lived. The search produces an unconventional autobiography almost devoid of the usual chronological, factual evidence; it concentrates on distilled experience and is based on first-hand contact with the indissoluble elements of mind and body as they are both observed over a long period and in their humdrum everyday activities. Though frequently inward-looking, the *Essais* also reflect late sixteenth-century attitudes refracted through the consciousness of a man who was both typical and untypical of his time.

Recognising that the search for absolute truth is beyond man's capacity, Montaigne seeks answers to more limited questions. What is the nature of the human condition? How should man behave in order to be happy? What is happiness or the supreme attainable good during our lifetime? How should man behave towards himself and towards his fellow-men? If the domain of his investigation is human, even in this circumscribed area, man must recognise the limitations of his intellectual faculties, the uncertainty of his senses and the deceptions of the emotions. Montaigne is keen on distinctions. Knowledge is useful only if it leads to a better life; reason is good only when used to achieve practical objectives such as living more at ease with one's conscience; custom and habit can be tyrannical if man becomes their slave, but a refuge from uncertainty where reason is powerless to find truth. In his search for answers to his own questions, Montaigne finally rejects all codes as being too rigid, but he takes from them what suits him and adapts them to his own purposes; he rejects authority, as he rejects everything which impinges on his freedom to judge according to his own criteria. He strives to expose all theories of behaviour which do not match his own experience of the complexity of reality.

Reality is, in this context, limited to what can be known with most certainty, that is, our own reactions, physical, emotional and intellectual, in practical situations. What is observed in this way after close inspection of the self is the only acceptable foundation for any conclusions about morality.

Introspection results in a proper appreciation of the human condition: mind and body are equally important and inseparable; we are made up of conflicting and changing emotions, which interact confusingly; the passions may sometimes deflect our reason but they are necessary to our harmonious functioning; they should be controlled not suppressed.

Education should lead not to more knowledge but to wisdom, which implies an ability to live according to a personally constructed scale of values. The means of achieving wisdom through education in the school of life is by the cultivation of one's judgement. This, for all its failings, is the key faculty which, for example, enables us to reject the false and the illusory (reputation and great deeds), to see the absurdity of *la chasse intellectuelle* or an unattainable moral code, to refuse total commitment. Positively, it makes us aware of the value of relativity, of moderation, teaches us that virtue is pleasurable, that adaptability and flexibility are essential provided they operate with the limits of our unchanging 'forme-maistresse'. When we take advantage of the fruits of experience, we are using our judgement to best effect; it will ensure that having discovered what allows us to live at peace with our conscience (which is a powerful force for good in all those who are 'bien nés') we will stand the best chance of pursuing and attaining that sense of 'repos' and 'tranquillité' which is at the summit of Montaigne's hierarchy of values. Provided only that inherent characteristics are not flawed at birth, education in its broad and narrow sense should be structured so as to give maximum scope for the development of individual potential, free from all restraint or compulsion.

The role of the cognitive faculties in Montaigne's psychological investigation of himself is a very positive one. If the principle of the acceptance of one's own 'forme-maistresse' seems passive, the task of discovering its nature is the result of a conscious decision and leads to a complex and intricate task of observation, analysis and judgement. Montaigne urges us not only to 'composer nos meurs' but also to be aware of the immense pleasure to be derived from every moment in life by the full involvement of our whole being, physical as well as intellectual.

Montaigne's attitude does not imply a rejection of all external obligation, merely an acceptance of only those obligations which are consistent with the full flowering of one's own potential. To cut oneself off from one's fellows would be an unacceptable impoverishment. We all have a duty to help others according to our talents provided we do not compromise our own inner serenity. Montaigne's lofty ideals about friendship and the actual relationship with La Boétie exemplify the former; his double term as elected mayor of Bordeaux demonstrates his belief in the latter.

This summary of some of the main ideas in the *Essais* is inevitably a distortion. Montaigne was right when he said 'tout abbregé sur un bon livre est un sot abregé' (III, 8, p.154B). The difficulties which faced Montaigne in writing the *Essais* also face anyone who tries to write about them: simplification of the subject matter is a falsification; rendering anything like its essential complexity runs the risk of being misunderstood.

With few exceptions the major themes of the *Essais* are liable to contain inconsistencies and contradictions over and above those which can be resolved in terms of chronological development. To complicate matters still further, it is impossible to deal with any single aspect of Montaigne in isolation. Each theme, each plane of meaning merges inextricably into the next. Paradoxes abound. Self-centred introspection leads to general propositions about human nature; within the pervading flux of human personality Montaigne clings to the certainty afforded by the 'forme-maistresse'; conservative attitudes jostle side by side with subversive, liberal ideas; a fierce attachment to the familiar, traditional and customary goes hand in hand with a flexibility of mind open to any new idea; the sceptic is also a

practising Catholic; a detached and penetrating intellect sometimes recommends 'incuriosité' and even ignorance; his
perception enables him to see similarities which others have
never guessed at, yet he is equally sharp at spotting distinctions
where others see only similarities; he commends a conversational, straightforward style but develops one of the most
complex and richly varied ever seen in literature; he speaks
scornfully of traditional forms of ordering a work but insists on
the deep unity of the *Essais*.

One of the great pleasures of increasing familiarity with the
Essais is to realise how these paradoxes, apparent and real, can
be made to fit together into a coherent whole. Montaigne's
labyrinthine multiplicity can be unified without distortion. The
key to the unity amid the multiplicity is the attempt by
Montaigne to convey his essence; this key itself is composed of a
whole series of many-faceted, volatile elements — in short, the
results of his introspection, in all their complexity, and the
complex artefact which he fashioned both to discover and
embody them. The potentially disparate reflections of a unique
but free-ranging spirit are transformed by Montaigne's
consummate artistry into a supremely satisfying, organic
creation which enriches those who study it and grow to admire it
on many different levels: intellectual, moral, psychological,
humanitarian, emotional and aesthetic.

The principle qualities for which I return to the *Essais*
so frequently are these. First, Montaigne's extraordinary
intelligence: it is both delicately discriminating and richly
suggestive. Not so much concerned with asserting the truth as
exploring all the possibilities, Montaigne is never afraid to admit
an error, that he has not found an answer or even that there is
not one to be found. Second, his awareness of the richness and
complexity of the human condition and his ability to suggest the
pleasure and dignity of life in all its physical, emotional and
intellectual manifestations without masking any of its
difficulties or limitations. Third, his refusal to accept illusory
goals or anything second hand, the freshness of his perception of
life, his unquenchable curiosity, the honesty of his introspection
and his ability to detect and deflate humbug. Finally, his

magnificently bold experiments in form and his multivalent style: he can be simple and elusive, homespun or philosophical, apparently effortless yet cunningly contrived. He is a master of manipulating various tones: familiar, humorous, conversational, serious, elegiac, ironically detached, subtly questioning but rarely pedantic; earthy anecdotes appear on the same page as classical references and rhetorical devices. He creates the illusion that he mirrors a whole life in his *Essais*.

Suggestions for Further Reading

Those who want to deepen and widen their knowledge of the *Essais* will soon realise the vast amount of material which is available. The problem, normally, is to know how best to use the limited time available and this may impose a rigorous definition of priorities. The suggestions which follow are based on what students of Montaigne have found profitable to read or dip into in the early stages of their acquaintance. Details of first editions and modern critical editions can be easily found in *1* below.

GENERAL WORKS

1. R.A. Sayce, *The Essays of Montaigne: A critical exploration* (Weidenfeld and Nicolson, London, 1972). This is the best book to read first; if one is the limit, this is it.

2. H. Friedrich, *Montaigne*, traduit par R. Rovini (Gallimard, Paris, 1968). An ideal complement to *1*.

SPECIALISED WORKS

Biography

3. D. Frame, *Montaigne: a biography* (Hamish Hamilton, London, 1965). This is the best biography.

Sources

4. P. Villey, *Les Sources et l'évolution des Essais de Montaigne*, 2nd edition revised, 2 vols (Hachette, Paris, 1933). Although dated in some respects, invaluable for sources and dating.

Style

5. M. McGowan, *Montaigne's deceits* (University Press, London, 1974). A perceptive, all-round treatment of Montaigne's attitude to style.

Background

6. P. Burke, *Montaigne* (Oxford University Press, Oxford, 1981). Short but admirable for setting Montaigne in the cultural context of the Renaissance.

Humanism

7. D. Frame, *Montaigne's discovery of man: the humanization of a humanist* (Columbia University Press, New York, 1955).

Scepticism

8. R.H. Popkin, *The History of Scepticism from Erasmus to Descartes*, revised edition (Harper and Row, London, 1968).

Politics

9. F. Brown, *Religious and Political Conservatism in the Essais of Montaigne* (Droz, Geneva, 1963).

Religion

10. H. Busson, *Le Rationalisme dans la littérature française de la Renaissance (1533-1601)* (Vrin, Paris, 1971). Chapters 13 and 14 especially.

Translation of the Essais

11. D. Frame, *The Complete Essays of Montaigne*, translated by D. Frame (Stanford University Press, California, 1965).

Other works by Montaigne

12. The *Journal de voyage*, letters and other items can be found in Montaigne, *Œuvres complètes*, edited by A. Thibaudet and M. Rat (Gallimard, Paris, 1962).

CRITICAL GUIDES TO FRENCH TEXTS

edited by
Roger Little, Wolfgang van Emden, David Williams